C000242492

Christianity in Close-up

Key Stage 3 RE

The Revelation of God

BOOK 1

Wendy Faris
Heather Hamilton

Colourpoint
Educational

© Wendy Faris, Heather Hamilton
and Colourpoint Books 2007

ISBN: 978 1 904242 75 8

First Edition
First Impression

Layout and design: Colourpoint Books
Printed by: W&G Baird Ltd

The acknowledgements on page 122 constitute an extension of this copyright page.

The New International Version of the Bible has been used throughout, unless otherwise stated.

Colourpoint Books
Colourpoint House
Jubilee Business Park
21 Jubilee Road
Newtownards
Co Down
BT23 4YH

Tel: 028 9182 0505
Fax: 028 9182 1900
E-mail: info@colourpoint.co.uk
Web site: www.colourpoint.co.uk

Wendy Faris BEd MSc teaches Religious Education to A2 level. In 2006 she was awarded a fellowship from the Farmington Trust (Ernst Cook fellow).

Heather Hamilton BEd also teaches Religious Education to A2 level. She is Head of Religious Education in Omagh Academy, County Tyrone, and has been teaching for 11 years.

All rights reserved. No part of this publication may be reproduced, stored in a retrieval system or transmitted in any form or by any means, electronic, mechanical, photocopying, scanning, recording or otherwise, without the prior written permission of the copyright owners and publisher of this book.

Contents

GUIDE TO ICONS

Activity

Discuss

Questions

Think

SKILLS AND CAPABILITIES KEY

Thinking Skills and Personal Capabilities*

- Com Communication
- ICT Using ICT
- Ma Using Maths
- MI Managing Information
- BC Being Creative
- TPD Thinking, Problem-solving, Decision-making
- SM Self-management
- WO Working with Others

Learning for Life and Work*

- EfE Education for Employability
- Cit Local and Global Citizenship
- PD Personal Development

* *These are suggestions only; you may be able to adapt activities further.*

God and the Bible

God's word

What is the Bible?

TPD
SM
Cit

Why do we have instructions?

What happens if we do not follow instructions?

What would the road be like without a Highway Code?

What would football be like without rules?

Com
MI
WO

What do you know about the Bible?

Copy out this diagram and write into the boxes things that you know about the Bible. You can add more boxes if you like.

Now share your ideas with a partner and add to your diagram.

Finally, share your ideas with the rest of the class.

What I know about the Bible

1

2

3

4

5

TPD
PD

These are some things people might say about the Bible.

Do you agree with any of these? Why, or why not?

It serves as a compass, mirror and lamp for life.

It has helped and encouraged people throughout history.

It is the best known book in the world.

It is available almost anywhere on Earth.

It has all the answers.

It has a message for people of every age.

The word 'Bible' comes from the Greek word '*biblos*' which means 'book'. The Bible is divided into two parts:

1 **The Old Testament**

2 **The New Testament**

The word '**testament**' means a **covenant** or an agreement. The Old Testament deals with the agreement made between God and man. The New Testament deals with the agreement made by God through Jesus Christ.

The Bible did not look like a book at first because books like the ones *we* know were not invented at the time it was written. It would have been written on **scrolls**. A scroll is a long piece of paper rolled up into a tube.

Sometimes scrolls were kept in stone jars.

Early copies of parts of the Old Testament were found amongst the **Dead Sea Scrolls**. These were found between 1947 and 1956, stored in stone jars.

These jars were hidden in caves along the shores of the Dead Sea in Israel. Some people think that the Dead Sea Scrolls prove that the words of the Old Testament have not changed much, even though they have been copied out by hand for hundreds and hundreds of years.

The Bible is not just one book but a whole collection of books.

The Old Testament is made up of 39 books.

There are more books which some Christians include in the Old Testament as well.

These extra books are sometimes called the **Apocrypha** and sometimes called the **Deuterocanonical** books.

There are 27 books in the New Testament.

Just like a real library, there are different types of books in the Bible. They are arranged into different sections. Each book is divided into chapters and each chapter is divided into verses.

When the Old Testament was first written, it was written in Hebrew because this was the language spoken in Israel. It is still spoken by the Israeli people today. Later the Old Testament was translated into Greek.

Most people think that the New Testament writers wrote their books in Greek. Others think that some parts of it were written in Hebrew. Greek was a language spoken all over the Roman Empire.

TPD

Bible trivia

1 What is the first book?

2 What is the last book?

3 How many books are there in the New Testament?

5 Find out which is the longest Psalm.

6 Find out which is the shortest Psalm.

The Greek alphabet

Α	α	Alpha
Β	β	Beta
Γ	γ	Gamma
Δ	δ	Delta
Ε	ε	Epsilon
Ζ	ζ	Zeta
Η	η	Eta
Θ	θ	Theta
Ι	ι	Iota
Κ	κ	Kappa
Λ	λ	Lambda
Μ	μ	Mu
Ν	ν	Nu
Ξ	ξ	Xi
Ο	ο	Omicron
Π	π	Pi
Ρ	ρ	Rho
Σ	σ	Sigma
Τ	τ	Tau
Υ	υ	Upsilon
Φ	φ	Phi
Χ	χ	Chi
Ψ	ψ	Psi
Ω	ω	Omega

TPD

The Greek connection

Many of our English words have a Greek connection.

They often start with a **prefix** eg, 'mono-' or 'micro-', and often end with the **suffix** '-logy' or '-graph' (or '-graphy').

One of your school subjects is one: geo***graphy***.

Can you think of any words which have the prefix 'mono-' or 'micro-'?

Later on, both the Old Testament and the New Testament were translated into Latin. From the sixteenth century onwards, the Bible has been translated into many different languages.

The Old Testament

The Old Testament books tell the story of the beginning of the universe and the creation of man.

We learn about brave men like Noah, David, Daniel and Moses and brave women like Ruth, Esther and Sarah.

Throughout the Old Testament, God asks his people to obey his laws, but over and over again his people disobey him. Despite this disobedience, God promises to make a way for all things to be right again.

After a break of about 400 years, the New Testament tells us how God's promise came true.

The Deuterocanonical books fill in some of the things that happened during these 400 years.

The New Testament

The New Testament brings us the story of the birth, life, death and resurrection of Jesus and the beginning and spread of the Christian Church.

The birth of Jesus Christ is an important event. Our dating system is based on it.

Before Jesus was born is known as **BC** (Before Christ). After Jesus was born is known as **AD**. In Latin this is *Anno Domini* and it means 'in the year of our Lord'.

MI
TPD
PD

The birth of a baby is a very special time.

Your birth was important.

In this task, think about the time before and the time after you were born.

Put two headings on a sheet of paper:

BEFORE I WAS BORN	AFTER I WAS BORN

Now write down important events under each heading. You might write things like these:

Man walked on the moon. My sister was born.	My granny celebrated her sixtieth birthday. The Nintendo Wii was produced.

More Bible trivia

- The Bible was the first book ever printed.
- The Bible has been translated in part or whole into over 2000 languages and dialects.
- The Bible was written in three different continents: Asia, Africa and Europe. It was written in many places: wilderness, prison, travelling, on islands ...
- Some people think that the Garden of Eden was in modern day Iraq and that Noah built his ark there.
- The shortest verse in the New International Version of the Bible is 'Jesus wept' in John 11:35.
- The longest verse is Esther 8:9.
- The longest word in the Bible is Maher-shalal-hash-baz (Isaiah 8:1).
- It is thought that the whole Bible can be read aloud in 70 hours.
- In 2 Samuel 21:20 we read of a man who had 12 fingers and 12 toes.
- There are 49 different types of food mentioned in the Bible. Almonds and pistachios are the only types of nuts mentioned (Genesis 43:11 and Numbers 19:8).
- Judges 20:16 mentions an army with 700 left-handed men.

The Bible library

Com
MI
TPD
Cit
PD

Thought shower

Do you go to a library sometimes?

Talk about libraries. What do you think they are for?

What was the last book you read?

Libraries are divided into different sections.

Why do you think this is?

The Bible is like a library because it has different sorts (*categories*) of books. A famous Christian called Jerome, who lived in the fourth and fifth centuries (300s and 400s), called the Bible a 'divine library'.

The categories of books in the Old Testament are:

Law	**eg Exodus**
History	**eg Joshua**
Poetry and Wisdom	**eg Job**
Prophecy	**eg Isaiah**

The categories of books in the New Testament are:

Gospel	**eg Luke**
History	**eg Acts**
Letters	**eg Galatians**
Prophecy	**eg Revelation**

TPD

What is a biography?

Can you think of any biographies of famous people?

Clue: Many well known footballers have biographies.

What is the difference between a biography and an autobiography?

MI
TPD

Look up each of the books in the first column below. Decide which category in the right hand column they belong to.

Book	Category
Genesis	wisdom
Psalms	history
1 Corinthians	prophecy
Proverbs	letter
Luke	poetry
Amos	Gospel

Bible referencing

When we have to find a particular place in the Bible we usually need to know the book, chapter and verse.

Example: Luke chapter 15 verse 1

People often shorten this in writing, for example:

Luke ch15 v1 or Luke 15:1

Com
MI
TPD
WO

Sword drill

In this game, the Bible is your sword.

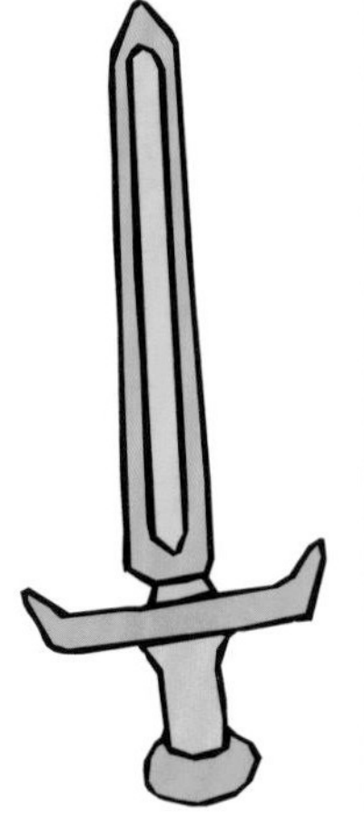

1 Sheath the sword! (Put the Bible under your arm)
2 Draw the sword! (Hold the Bible in your hand above you)
3 Listen to the reference called out by your teacher, for example Acts 1:8. Repeat the reference after your teacher.
4 Charge! When your teacher gives this command you should find the verse as quickly as you can!

The first one to find it is the winner.

Why not have a class competition?

The story of the Bible

If you want to write a story all you have to do is to go to a shop and buy an exercise book, a pen, and then begin. You might even word process it.

In ancient times things were very different. People had to make their own writing materials.

BC
TPD

If you could not go to a shop, do you think you could make your own materials to write on and pens to write with?

Think about how you might do it.

TPD
MI

Look up these references and find the information asked for.

John 20:24: one of the twelve disciples

Genesis 23:2: Abraham's wife died here

1 Kings 17:1: A great prophet

1 Kings 3:9: Solomon prayed for this

Luke 22:39: A hill

Genesis 24:67: Isaac's wife

1 Samuel 16:13: He became a great king

Acts 23:24: a Roman governor

Mark 1:39: Jesus came from this area

Colossians 4:1: a slave

Acts 9:3: Saul went here

Now take the first letter of each answer. What does it spell out about the Bible?

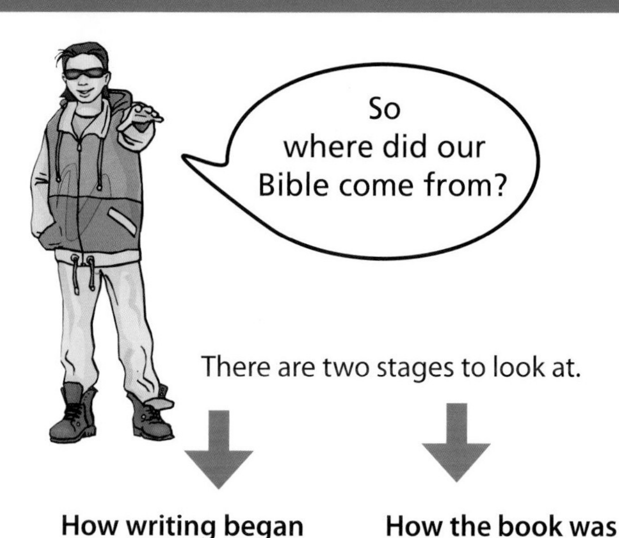

There are two stages to look at.

How writing began | **How the book was developed**

HOW WRITING BEGAN

People did not always write using words. Thousands of years ago, symbols and signs were used instead.

At the time when Old Testament events took place, stories were passed on by word of mouth from generation to generation. We call this the **oral tradition**.

BC TPD WO Cit PD

Sometimes today we use signs and symbols instead of words.

With a partner, make a list of five signs we use today.

Why do we use signs instead of writing?

What would your journey to school be like without signs and symbols?

Design a sign of your own which could be used in school, eg 'No running in the corridors' or 'No eating and drinking in class'.

Com BC PD

Many of the things we buy have signs and symbols on them. They are there to help us.

Look at the label inside a piece of clothing, eg your school sweater. Now copy the symbols and write beside them what they mean.

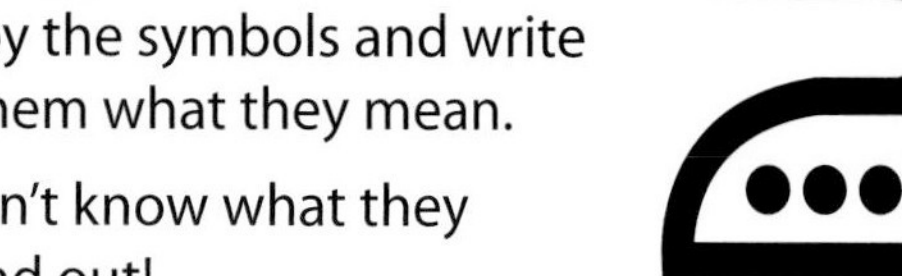

If you don't know what they mean, find out!

Com Ma MI TPD

Crack the code

If A = 1 B = 2 C = 3, can you finish the code? Write it out.

Now try to fill in the words where the numbers are in this passage.

Where did the European and Middle-Eastern alphabets come from?

Many thousands of years ago 16 18 5 8 9 19 20 15 18 9 3 men painted pictures of animals, birds and men on cave walls. This was the first kind of writing.

About 5000 years ago, a simple writing system using 16 9 3 20 15 7 18 1 16 8 19 was developed in ancient Mesopotamia (an area that today includes Iraq, parts of Syria, Turkey and Iran).

These pictographs were pressed into 19 15 6 20 3 12 1 25 that could then be baked into hard tablets and stored.

Gradually this developed into an 1 12 16 8 1 2 5 20.

Meanwhile, the Egyptians were using a picture language called 8 9 5 18 15 7 12 25 16 8 9 3 19.

These formed the basis of an alphabet that appeared in Canaan (modern Israel) in the second millennium BC. All modern alphabets, including the 8 5 2 18 5 23 and Arabic alphabets, probably came from this.

FROM CLAY TO BOOKS

Writing boards were used by the Assyrians and were common in Greek and Roman times. They were made of wood or ivory with a wax surface for writing. Often two boards were hinged together.

Parchment The skins of sheep or goats were cleaned and polished. This made a smooth surface for writing on.

Papyrus This was made from the stems of a reed called papyrus which grew along the River Nile in Egypt. The stems were cut into thin strips. These were laid side by side, overlapping, on a hard surface. The layers were soaked and then beaten with mallets and dried. This made flat sheets. Sheets were stuck together to make **scrolls**.

Papyrus was expensive for ordinary people and so they often used broken bits of pottery for small notes, bills and receipts. Lots of these have been found in Egypt.

Codex The scroll was replaced by the codex around the second century AD (100s). A codex was made up of sheets of parchment or papyrus folded and fastened together at one side so that it opened like a book. Sometimes it had a cover as well.

The codex made it easier to find a particular passage. It was also easier to store.

A very famous codex is the **Codex Siniaticus**. It was written in Greek in the fourth century AD. It is the earliest manuscript of the New Testament.

COPIES AND TRANSLATIONS

By the third century BC, many Jews were living in countries around the Mediterranean as well as in Israel.

For many of these Jews, their first language was not Hebrew. They spoke Greek so they needed to be able to read the scriptures in their own language.

A translation of the Old Testament from Hebrew into Greek was begun in the third century BC.

Around the sixth century AD the Jews decided that they wanted a single version of their scriptures so that Jews all over the world would be reading the same thing. They gathered together all the different copies and removed any differences.

The men who were given the job of writing this new text were called the **Massoretes**. This work was carried out between the sixth and tenth centuries AD.

MI
TPD

This Greek translation was called the **Septuagint**, which is Latin for seventy.

That's an unusual name for a manuscript.

Find out one reason why people think it got its name.

Once the Old Testament was translated into Greek, do you think the Jews would be the only ones to read it?

Who else might have been very interested to read it?

BC
SM
WO
PD

Make an exact copy of Psalm 121.

Take your time and copy out each word carefully, one at a time.

Get a partner to check your copy.

Did you make any mistakes?

How hard was it to keep your concentration?

How long did it take to copy out the whole Psalm?

How is the Bible used?

iStockphoto/Bobbie Osborne

1 Individual reading

Many Christians feel that reading the Bible regularly at home helps them to understand more about God and the ways he wants them to live their lives.

Christians often read the Bible slowly so that the meaning becomes clearer. A Bible passage can guide or help them.

iStockphoto/Sean Warren

2 Reading in groups

Christians often come together in small groups to study the Bible. This means they share what they learn with each other.

THE BIBLE IN PUBLIC WORSHIP AND CEREMONIES

Christians read the Bible for guidance and encouragement because they feel it helps them in every situation in life. They believe it is God's word – God speaking to his people.

"Your word is a lamp to my feet and a light for my path"

Psalm 119:105

1. Parts of the Bible are usually read aloud during a church service. In some churches people remain standing during a reading to show respect.
2. Passages from the Bible are read during ceremonies like baptisms, weddings and funerals.

iStockphoto/Courtney Navey

Com MI BC

What is your experience of the Bible or Bible stories?

If you have ever heard or read a Bible story or listened to passages read in school or in church, pick one and write about it.

Then write a few sentences explaining why you remembered this particular story.

HOW DID THE BOOKS OF THE BIBLE COME TOGETHER?

How were the Old Testament books collected?

Stage 1	People told their children the stories.
Stage 2	The stories were written down.
Stage 3	The Ten Commandments given to Moses were kept in a special box called the Ark of the Covenant.
Stage 4	Poems and Psalms were collected and used in Temple worship.
Stage 5	A complete collection of books was arranged.
Stage 6	The Books of the Old Testament were agreed in AD90.

This is one idea of what the Ark of the Covenant might have looked like.

How were the New Testament books collected?

Stage 1	The disciples of Jesus told people about him.
Stage 2	The Apostle Paul and other men in the early Christian church wrote letters to the churches.
Stage 3	Many Christians were being put to death for believing in Jesus. Also, time was passing since Jesus lived on Earth. So it was decided that the stories about him should be written down. These stories were called the Gospels.
Stage 4	The Gospels and letters were collected together.

Books, glorious books!

- The Bible is the world's best-selling book.
- It holds the world record for paperback sales.
- It has been translated into more languages than any other book.
- The Bible, and parts of it, hold records for the most expensive book ever sold. For instance, the Gutenberg Bible (one of the first printed Bibles) was sold for £1,265,000 at auction in 1978.
- A book containing part of the Bible is the most expensive book ever sold. A 12th century book containing the Gospels was auctioned in London in 1983. It was sold for about £8 million!

TPD

Thought shower

Why do you think some books become bestsellers?

Why do you think the Bible became a bestseller?

Ma MI BC TPD PD

Think about a book that you have enjoyed. Write a review of it.

Say:

- who wrote it
- when it was written
- what you enjoyed about it
- what, if anything, could have made the book even better
- the rating out of 10 you would give the book (with 10 being the best)

BC
TPD

Design a poster to boost sales of the Bible.

Think about who the book was written for, the content of the book and how the cover should be presented.

Who wrote the Bible?

Christians believe that God works through people. He chose ordinary individuals and groups and worked in their lives so that they learned important truths about him through the things that happened.

Many people were involved in writing the Bible and we can't know who they all were.

The table below has information about some of the people we can be fairly sure about.

MOSES	Born an Israelite slave in Egypt. Adopted by an Egyptian princess and brought up in the Royal household. Moses led the Israelites out of Egypt. He wrote down the Ten Commandments.
DAVID	A shepherd boy who became Israel's most celebrated King. He wrote many of the Psalms.
LUKE	A doctor and friend of Paul. He wrote Luke and Acts.
MATTHEW	A tax collector who was very unpopular. He became a disciple of Jesus and probably wrote the Gospel of Matthew.
JOHN	He was a fisherman along with his brother James. As well as writing the Gospel of John, he also wrote three letters and the Book of Revelation.

Com
MI
TPD

These sentences are jumbled up. Rewrite them so that they make sense.

1 Psalms David of wrote the many
2 Luke books two wrote New Testament Acts called Luke and
3 was an collector disciple tax of who Matthew unpopular became Jesus a
4 prophet was a shepherd Amos became who a
5 were fishermen and James John
6 boy David of Israel a was King shepherd became who
7 used God ordinary people Bible write to the

Inside the New Testament

MI
TPD
PD

Look up and write out the passages below.

Think of some situations where a Christian might find them helpful.

Hebrews 13:5-6	Romans 8:28
1 Peter 5:7	Proverbs 3:5-6

BOOKS OF POETRY AND WISDOM

The Books of Poetry and Wisdom are Job, Psalms, Proverbs, Ecclesiastes and Song of Songs.

Com
MI
TPD
WO
PD

Can you think of any wise sayings?

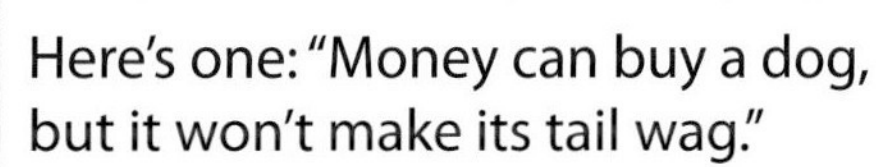

Here's one: "Money can buy a dog, but it won't make its tail wag."

The Book of Proverbs is full of sayings.

Read parts of the Book of Proverbs and pick out sayings that you particularly like. Write down their chapter and verse references.

In turn, read one out to the class. Say why you like it.

MI
TPD

Join up the beginning and ending of these sayings from Proverbs.

Proverbs 13:24 He who spares the rod hates his son	but a poor man's friends desert him.
Proverbs 19:4 Wealth brings many friends	but diligent hands bring wealth.
Proverbs 16:18 Pride goes before destruction	but a kind word cheers him up.
Proverbs 12:18 Reckless words pierce like a sword	but he who loves him is careful to discipline him.
Proverbs 10:4 Lazy hands make a man poor	so drop the matter before a dispute breaks out.
Proverbs 17:14 Starting a quarrel is like breaching a dam	a haughty spirit before a fall.
Proverbs 12:25 An anxious heart weighs a man down	and in the end you will be wise.
Proverbs 19:20 Listen to advice and accept instruction	but the tongue of the wise brings healing.
Proverbs 20:19 A gossip betrays a confidence	keeps himself from calamity.
Proverbs 21:23 He who guards his mouth and his tongue	so avoid a man who talks too much.

THE GOSPELS

The first four books of the New Testament are **Matthew**, **Mark**, **Luke** and **John** and are known as the gospels, which means 'Good News'. They include what Jesus did and what he said.

Without Jesus the New Testament would never have been written. He lived for only about 33 years in a small country but he changed the world. He has probably had more influence than anyone in history.

The Gospels were written by four different people so they all tell the story from a different point of view. Some things which Jesus said or did are included in one Gospel and not in another but all the main events in his life are the same in each Gospel.

All four gospels agree that Jesus was from Nazareth in Galilee. When he was about 30, he was baptised in the River Jordan by John the Baptist. For the next three years he travelled around preaching and teaching and healing many people. Christians believe he brought the good news that anyone who believed in him and told God that they were sorry for the wrong things they did would be part of God's kingdom.

Jesus was unpopular with a lot of people because he said and did things that went against the traditional religious teachings of the time. He was sentenced to death because of this.

According to the gospels Jesus was seen alive three days after his death. This event is known as the **Resurrection** and is very important for Christians. The whole of the Christian faith is built on this.

After the four gospels comes **Acts**. Its full name is the *Acts of the Apostles* because it describes the acts (actions) of the Apostles. Apostle is another word for disciple. Acts records the spread of the Christian Church throughout the Roman Empire.

We learn about the adventures of Peter and Paul. Paul had tried to kill Christians before he became a Christian himself.

Peter and Paul wrote letters to the people in the cities which they had visited. There are many letters that answer questions about the Christian life. Some of these letters follow Acts in the New Testament. There are also letters by others, eg Jude and James.

The last book is **Revelation**. Its full name is the *Revelation of John the Divine*. Many people think that this was John, Jesus' disciple and the same man who wrote the gospel of John. He wrote Revelation when he was an old man. It is not an easy book to understand. John describes many visions that he had.

MI

1 What is a Gospel?
2 Which books in the New Testament are Gospels?
3 What is the most important event in the New Testament?
4 What is the Book of Acts about?
5 Why did Jesus' followers write letters to the people in the cities they had visited?

THE BIBLE AROUND THE WORLD

MI

Key developments in the translation of the Bible worldwide

Copy the following sentences putting in the missing words as you go.

Pick from the words below.

1 Sometime between AD383 to 405 a monk called Jerome translated the Bible into _____ because this was the language used by most people in Rome and Western Europe at this time.
2 The first complete version of the Bible in English was produced by _________ in the late 14th century.
3 Books started to be printed in the ________ century making them cheaper. This meant that people could have their own copy of the Bible and read it for themselves.
4 The _________________ of the Bible was printed in 1611.
5 The ______________ was introduced in 1966.
6 In 1976 the ________________ was made available.
7 In 1978 the _________________ version appeared.

New International Version; Jerusalem Bible; King James Version; Good News Bible; Fifteenth; John Wycliffe; Latin

TPD

Thoughtshower

How many versions of the Bible can you name?

Com TPD Cit

A tricky translation challenge

Can you work out the contents of this passage from a French version of the New Testament? Do any words look familiar?

Jésus étant né à Bethléhem en Judée, au temps du roi Hérode, voici des mages d'Orient arrivèrent à Jérusalem, et dirent: Où est le roi des Juifs qui vient de naître? car nous avons vu son étoile en Orient, et nous sommes venus pour l'adorer.

Matthew 2:1-2 Louis Segond

Com BC WO PD

Mime

Some of you will be given cards with different occupations or emotions on them. Mime these to the rest of the class. They have to 'translate' what you are doing.

You must not show your card to anyone else. Afterwards, discuss the following questions in class:

1 Which mime was the most difficult and why?
2 What difficulties do you think Bible translators have?

The Bible – A book worth dying for?

TPD PD

Is there anything you feel so strongly about that you would take risks to support it?

The Latin Bible was used in churches for hundreds of years but people gradually stopped speaking Latin. When this happened, they relied on priests to read the Bible and tell them what was in it. Eventually, people were not happy with having only a Latin Bible. They wanted the Bible in their own language so that they could read and understand it for themselves.

Many people tried to translate the Bible into English. **John Wycliffe** and **William Tyndale** are two of the most famous.

JOHN WYCLIFFE

John Wycliffe was the first person who decided to translate the whole Bible into English so that ordinary people could read it. He didn't think that priests should be able to decide what parts of the Bible to read out and how to interpret it.

Wycliffe began leading the translation in 1380. There was no printing in those days so each Bible had to be copied out by hand.

It is thought that each copy took about ten months to produce.

The church at this time had become **corrupt** and many of its leaders had become rich. Groups of Christians all over Europe began to protest against some of the teachings and practices of the church.

Many church leaders did not want ordinary people to read the Bible for themselves. Some were afraid that ordinary, untrained people would interpret the Bible wrongly.

The church leaders banned Wycliffe's translation. They called his followers **Lollards** and said they were teaching against the practices of the Church.

Many people read Wycliffe's Bible in secret because they were afraid of being punished. Some of the Lollards were tortured, and it is said that some were burned to death, with their Bibles tied around their necks.

BC

Draw a 'Wanted' poster for Wycliffe and his translators.

THE GIDEONS INTERNATIONAL

TPD

The Gideons give out Bibles to Year 8 pupils. Perhaps you already have one.

Who are the Gideons and why do they give out Bibles?

How the Gideons began

John Nicholson was only 12 when his mother died. She asked him to promise her that he would pray and read the Bible every day.

Years later John was working as a travelling salesman when he met two other Christian salesmen, Will Knights and Samuel Hill. They formed the Gideons Association in 1899 in Wisconsin, USA.

Soon the association began placing Bibles in hotel rooms so that business people and holiday-makers could read them if they wanted to. They went on to leave Bibles in prisons, universities, hospitals, and ships, amongst other places.

They also began visiting schools to give out copies of the New Testament and Psalms to young people. They hoped that these young people would read God's word and become Christians.

The Gideons take their name from the story of Gideon in the Bible. In this story, to show his power, God reduced Gideon's army from 32,000 men to only 300. This small number of men then went on to beat a much larger enemy force.

A Gideon Bible which was given out at school.

The Gideon Association began with only three men relying on God. In the Bible, Gideon's army went into battle with the cry "A sword for the Lord". Today, Gideons rely on God's word, which the Bible sometimes calls the "Sword of the Spirit".

ICT
TPD
PD

What more would you like to know about the Gideons?

If you could talk to a member of the Gideons Association, what would you ask them?

Do you think they are brave?

Find out more about the Gideons from their website:

www.gideons.org.uk

Members of the Gideon Association handing out Bibles at a school.

The association now has more than 250,000 members in 180 countries. They give out 120 copies of the Bible every minute!

TPD

Badge of the Gideons

Read the story of Gideon in Judges 6-7.

What do you think the symbols on the badge might mean?

MI
TPD
Cit

Find Wisconsin on a map of the United States.

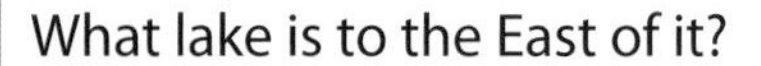

What lake is to the East of it?

MARY JONES

Mary Jones lived about 200 years ago. She was a poor Welsh girl who loved to hear stories from the Bible, but Bibles in the Welsh language were rare and expensive.

When Mary went to school and learned to read she began to want her own Bible.

She saved up her money for six years so that she would have enough to buy one. When she was 15, she had saved up enough money. She walked, barefoot, for 25 miles to the town of Bala to buy her Bible.

She was exhausted by the time she arrived at the home of a man called Thomas Charles and asked for a Bible to buy. According to one version of the story, all his Bibles were either sold out or promised to other people. However, Mary was so upset that he gave her one of the Bibles that was meant for someone else.

Later, at a meeting, Thomas Charles spoke about the need for Bibles in Welsh. So, in 1804, the British and Foreign Bible Society was formed. Its aim was to provide Bibles for people all over the world, in their own languages, as cheaply as possible. The organisation is now known as the Bible Society.

It was not long before other Bible Societies were being formed throughout the world.

BIBLE SOCIETIES

Wycliffe International

William Cameron Townsend was an American missionary who went to Central America in the early 1900s. While he was living with the Cakchiquel Indians in Guatemala, one man asked him: "If your God is so great, why doesn't he speak my language?"

Immediately William Townsend set about seeing what could be done to show the man that God did understand his language. He began translating the New Testament into Cakchiquel.

He realised that there was a need for Bibles in many other languages so he founded Camp Wycliffe in 1934, which grew into the Wycliffe Bible Translators in 1942.

Since 1934 Wycliffe workers have helped to complete 710 translations, making the Bible available to approximately 78 million people. It takes a long time and can take anywhere from five to 20 years to produce a New Testament alone.

Wycliffe has 6,600 members in over 70 countries. According to Wycliffe, there are still 2,200 languages which may need translations.

A Wycliffe worker in Papa New Guinea, translating the Gospel of Luke into Bilau.

VIEWS ABOUT THE BIBLE

The Old Testament is important to Christians as they believe it is the inspired word of God and forms the first part of the Bible. Christianity began in Judaism so the Old Testament is an important link between Jews and Christians. It contains God's laws for society, eg the Commandments.

The Old Testament is important to Jews because it contains the story of their history and their laws.

The New Testament is important to Christians because it outlines Jesus' life from his birth to the resurrection. It gives advice to Christians and it tells the story of how Christianity began.

Jews do not accept the New Testament because they do not believe Jesus was the Messiah/Son of God.

MI TPD

Copy and complete the diagram below.

Think about the views Christians and Jews have about the Bible.

In the middle, list the similarities in their views about it. On the outside, list the differences.

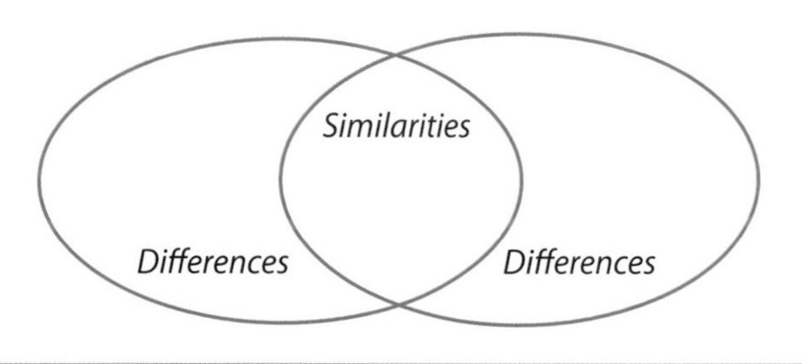

TPD PD

Thoughtshower

Have a brainstorm on the topic of bravery. Try to give modern examples as well as examples from the Bible.

Com TPD PD

Have you ever had to be brave?

Share with the rest of the class a time when you showed bravery.

BROTHER ANDREW

Brother Andrew was someone who showed great bravery.

Brother Andrew's real name is Andy van der Biji. He was born in 1928 and grew up in a village about 20 miles north of Amsterdam in the Netherlands. When he was 12 years old the Germans bombed and invaded the Netherlands and things became very difficult.

By the time the war was over he was 17 years old and he had to get a job. A war was going on between the Netherlands and Indonesia so Brother Andrew became a soldier. He actually had to kill people and he didn't like this. When he wasn't fighting he used to get drunk with his friends. Their motto was: 'Be smart, go crazy'.

Then one day Brother Andrew was shot in the ankle, smashing it. It seemed as if he would never walk properly again. He had a lot of time to think while he was in hospital. The nurses were nuns and were always cheerful and kind. They told Brother Andrew how God helped them do their jobs. This reminded him of his mother who had recently died. She had believed very strongly in God. Brother Andrew started to read the pocket Bible his mother had given him.

He went back to the Netherlands and was sent to a training camp for injured soldiers. He ended up going to a Christian meeting. He started to pray and read his Bible more often. He promised to follow God if God would show him the way. This was the beginning of Brother Andrew's new life.

He began working in a chocolate factory and he told everyone there about Jesus. What he really wanted was to become a missionary but he was worried about his ankle which was still sore. One day he decided to become a missionary in spite of his ankle and after this it got better. Brother Andrew believed that God had healed him.

Andrew went to Bible school. After he had finished studying there in 1955, Brother Andrew felt that God was calling him to go to Poland and Russia. These were communist countries at the time. In a communist country no-one was allowed to become rich by owning a business. The government owned all the shops, factories and farms and paid the workers. Christians were persecuted for their faith in these countries.

Brother Andrew visited churches in these countries and discovered that they needed Bibles. He made up his mind to take them as many Bibles as he could. He used his car to smuggle some Bibles over the borders, praying that the guards wouldn't find them. If they had, they would have taken them away.

The work that Brother Andrew was doing developed gradually into a worldwide organisation called Open Doors. Open Doors has brought Bibles and help to Christians all over the world, including Eastern Europe, the Middle East, China and Latin America.

Their work often has to be secret because it would not be allowed in the countries they work in. Brother Andrew has become known as 'God's Smuggler'. This is also the name of his best-selling autobiography.

TPD WO Cit PD

Read Mark 12:17.

In groups, discuss whether you think it is right to smuggle Bibles, against the law of the country.

Each group should report back to the whole class, giving reasons for your decision.

ICT

Websearch

You can find out more about the work Open Doors does today from the website www.opendoors.org.uk

Find out where in the world today Christians face the greatest threat of persecution.

Com TPD WO PD

Have a class debate around the following statement:

"The Bible is old fashioned, out of date and is not relevant in modern society."

Holy Writings

Christianity is not the only religion to have a holy book. Hinduism has many holy books which are divided into two categories, **Smriti** and **Shruti**. Shruti are scriptures that Hindus believe were revealed directly by God. Smriti are in the form of stories. Hindu holy writings are in the Sanskrit language.

A scene from the Mahabharata

(Smriti writings)

The **Tanach**, or Hebrew Bible, is the Jewish holy book and is included in the Old Testament of the Christian Bible. An important section is the **Torah**, the first five books of the Tanach. Can you name them?

The **Qur'an** is the Muslim holy book. Muslims believe it was revealed to the prophet Muhammad (PBUH) by the angel Jibril (Gabriel). The Qur'an is written in Arabic.

Pages of the Qur'an

MI Cit

Can you find out the names of the holy writings of other world faiths?

eg Buddhism, Sikhism and the Bahá'í faith.

God's relationship with his chosen people

Abraham

Abraham means 'father of a multitude'. Sometimes the Bible refers to Abraham as 'Abram' and to Sarah as 'Sarai'.

Abram and Sarai were their original names but God changed them when he made his covenant or promise with Abraham.

ABRAHAM'S JOURNEY

Abraham was born near the city of **Ur** around 2000BC. His father was called Terah.

From Ur, Abraham and his family moved to **Haran**, about 600 miles to the northwest. They were **nomadic** tribesmen and they followed the weather and the best sources of food, so this may explain why they moved to Haran. While they lived there, the Bible tells us that Terah died at the age of 205.

GOD'S COVENANT WITH ABRAHAM

When Abraham was 75 and still living in Haran, God called him to obey his commands. This was Abraham's **vocation**.

TPD PD

Some people in the world today feel that they have received a vocation or calling from God.

What do you think God might call people to do?

Read about the covenant in Genesis 12:1-3.

This agreement or promise was part of God's covenant with Abraham. The covenant was really a contract – Abraham had to fulfil his part of the agreement and God had to fulfil his part.

TPD

Can you think of any modern day contracts or covenants?

The pictures will give you some ideas.

Abraham is regarded as the **forefather** of the Jewish nation. Because of this covenant, Jews are often seen as God's chosen people.

A covenant or contract works only if both parties keep their side of the bargain. It wasn't easy for Abraham to do all the things that God had asked. He didn't have an easy way to travel and he was also very old.

Read Genesis 12:1 again. Do you think that there was anything else that made it difficult for Abraham to obey God?

Abraham needed a lot of faith to obey God. But what is faith?

TPD WO PD

What do you think faith is? Write it down.

Give your definition to a partner and ask them what they think of it.

Charles Blondin

On 30 June 1859, Charles Blondin crossed the Niagara Falls on a tightrope, about 70 metres above the water.

When he had done it, he asked all the people watching if they thought he could do it carrying a man on his back. The audience cheered and shouted "Yes"! But when he asked for a volunteer they went quiet.

His agent, Henry Colcord, agreed to go. Colcord was carried successfully across the Falls.

TPD PD

Talk about what Blondin did.

Why did Henry Colcord agree to be carried over?

Would you have volunteered to be carried over?

MI TPD

Bible search

Look up Hebrews 11:1 and write out the verse.

Is this a good definition of faith?

ICT MI BC

Investigation

Research someone who has shown a lot of faith. It could be Christian faith, faith in another religion, faith in science etc.

Then complete a profile of their life, including the following details:

- Name
- Time when they lived or their age now
- What they had faith in
- How they showed their faith
- Their achievements (if any)
- Any other interesting information

You could word process your profile and include some pictures.

ABRAHAM DOUBTS GOD'S PROMISE

MI TPD

Look again at the first promise God made to Abraham in Genesis 12:2. Now read Genesis 15:2.

Do you think that Abraham may have started to doubt God's promise? Explain your answer.

Sarah was not able to have children and she was now an old woman. This was a great shame in Jewish society at the time as it was seen as a punishment from God.

But then God made a wonderful promise. God said that if they obeyed him they would have a son.

It became really difficult for Abraham and Sarah to have faith. God had spoken to Abraham and established the covenant when he was 75 years old. Now Abraham was 86 and they still did not have a child.

Sarah started to worry that Abraham would die before they had any children so she and Abraham did something wrong.

MI
TPD

Read the story in Genesis 16 :1-16 and answer these questions.

1 What nationality was Sarah's maidservant?

2 How did Hagar's attitude towards Sarah change when she became pregnant?

3 What did Hagar do when Sarah mistreated her?

4 What was the name of Abraham and Hagar's son?

5 Do you think that God punished Abraham for sleeping with Hagar?

GOD REASSURES ABRAHAM

One day three men visited Abraham. He thought they were travellers who were passing through the country. Abraham invited the strangers to come in to rest and to have something to eat.

But while they were there, God told Abraham that he would soon have a son. Sarah was standing in the door of the tent when she heard this. She laughed as she thought it impossible for her to have a child at her age.

However she did have a son. They called him Isaac, which means 'laughter'. Genesis tells us Abraham was 100 years old when Isaac was born.

ISAAC AND ISHMAEL

BC
WO
PD

Think of this story as an episode of a television soap opera, and you have to write a scene for it.

The situation is that Isaac is born and Ishmael is a young boy. Hagar and Sarah are living side by side with two children. Abraham is the father of both. What is the atmosphere in the camp like?

How do Hagar and Sarah feel towards each other?

Now use your imagination and write a scene.

When you have written it, members of your class could act it out.

After Isaac was born, Sarah started to think that if Abraham died Ishmael would try to claim part of the inheritance. She didn't want this because she wanted Isaac to inherit everything. So she made Abraham send Hagar and Ishmael away from the camp into the desert.

Hagar wandered through the desert until she ran out of water. She thought that Ishmael was going to die and she could not bear to watch, so she put him down under a tree. She then sat down nearby and began to cry in despair.

God heard Hagar and spoke to her. He told her not to be afraid, because Ishmael would grow up to be the leader of a great nation. God then gave Hagar water and she and Ishmael survived.

Many people believe that, as he had promised, God made Ishmael the father of the Arab nation. Others don't think this is right.

GOD TESTS ABRAHAM'S FAITH

TPD
SM
PD

Think of a time in your life when you wanted something very, very much.

If you eventually got what you wanted, do you remember how you felt ?

How would you have felt if it was suddenly taken away from you?

TPD

Sacrifice

What does the word 'sacrifice' mean? Draw a thought bubble and write your ideas inside it.

In the Old Testament, people offered animal sacrifices to God so that they could have their sins forgiven. To be good enough to sacrifice, the animal had to be perfect. In other words, it had to be of real value to them. An old or sick animal cost them nothing and was not a real sacrifice to God.

Christians no longer offer animal sacrifices to God, because they believe that Jesus became the final sacrifice to take away people's sins.

TPD SM PD

Write down three people who make sacrifices for you. Explain how they make a sacrifice.

If you were asked to give a sacrifice to God, what would you give?

Explain your choice.

Cit PD

Many people think that rich countries should try and help poorer countries.

What sacrifices could people in rich countries make to help people in poorer countries?

Have you ever tried to help in any of these ways?

Abraham and Sarah had always wanted a son and were very happy when Isaac was born. You can imagine how much they loved him.

Then God decided that he was going to test Abraham. He wanted to see how much faith Abraham had.

MI BC

Read the story in Genesis 22:1-14.

Now write an account of what happened.

Use the writing frame to help you.

God came to Abraham and said …
Abraham obeyed God and the next day …
Isaac carried … and Abraham carried …
Isaac was confused because … but Abraham said …
When they reached Mount Moriah …
God spoke from heaven saying …
Abraham then saw …

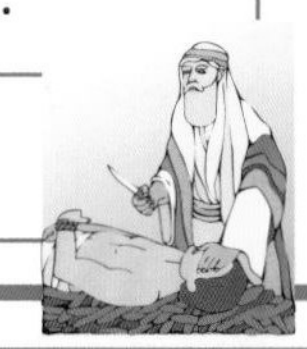

Com BC

Imagine you are Isaac. Write a diary entry for the day you went with your father to offer a sacrifice to God.

Really try to *be* Isaac and tell all the things that happened and what you were feeling at the time.

Ages in the Bible

The oldest man in the Bible lived 969 years. His name was Methusaleh. That's why we use the expression "as old as Methusaleh".

But did he live 969 years?

Different ways were used to work out time when the Old Testament was written.

A year could have been based on:

the sun

or how long a King ruled

Letters in the Hebrew and Greek alphabets were also used as numbers. Because some letters looked almost the same, mistakes in copying could have been made.

A WIFE FOR ISAAC

TPD SM PD

Would you like it if your parents arranged who you could go out with?

Why or why not?

Arranged marriages still sometimes happen today within some religions, eg Hinduism and Islam.

Isaac grew up and eventually the time came for him to marry.

Abraham wanted to make sure that he had a good wife, so he sent his head servant in search of a suitable girl.

Read Genesis 24 to discover who was chosen to marry Isaac.

Sarah died when she was 127 and Abraham married again and had 6 more sons.

Abraham died when he was 175. (Genesis 25:7)

JACOB AND ESAU

Isaac and Rebekah got married and had twin boys. Genesis 25:24-28 tells us that Esau was the first twin to be born and that he had reddish, hairy skin. Jacob was quite the opposite – he was fair-skinned.

Unfortunately it was not a happy home – each of the parents had a favourite. Esau loved the outdoor life and he was a skilled hunter so Isaac favoured Esau. He loved to eat the animals Esau hunted.

Jacob grew up to be a quiet man who liked to stay at home and help his mother around the tents. Rebekah favoured Jacob.

TPD Cit PD

1 Do you think it is fair for parents to have favourites?

2 If they do, what sort of problems can this cause?

The Birthright

As Esau was the elder son he owned the **birthright**. This meant that when his father died, Esau would inherit two shares of all Isaac's property and wealth. Even more importantly, he also would become the head of the family, which meant a lot of privileges and responsibility.

Jacob was angry, as this meant he would only receive one share of the inheritance. He was jealous of Esau and he planned to get the birthright for himself.

Unfortunately Esau did not respect the birthright and one day he gave it away.

Com BC WO

Read the story of what happened in Genesis 25:29-34.

Now split into pairs. One of you should take the side of Esau, and the other Jacob.

Each of you should write a diary entry for this day. When you have finished, read each other's entries and talk about the differences in how each brother felt about what happened.

Jacob steals Esau's Blessing

At this time, before a father died he would bless his eldest son. This was a sign that he was passing responsibility for the family to him. Isaac knew that he was getting old, so he decided it was time to give Esau the blessing.

Read Genesis 27:1-45 to find out what happened.

BC TPD SM Cit PD

Happy families

No family is happy all the time.

Write down five reasons why teenagers and their parents might argue.

Write down five things that were wrong with Isaac and Rebekah's family.

Now, write down five rules which you think are important for a happy family.

Discuss these in class.

JACOB AND RACHEL

You can imagine how afraid and worried Jacob was as he made his way to Haran to the home of his uncle, Laban.

One night when Jacob stopped to rest he had a very strange dream. In the dream he saw a ladder reaching from earth to heaven. Angels were going up and down the ladder, and God was at the top of it.

In the dream God made a covenant or agreement with Jacob. God promised that:

- he would give Jacob many descendents
- he would give them the land on which Jacob was lying
- he would bless them

When Jacob woke up the next morning he built an altar to show his thanks to God .

Jacob arrived in Haran and began to work for his uncle Laban. He fell in love with Laban's youngest daughter, Rachel.

One day Laban told Jacob it wasn't fair that Jacob should work for him for nothing. He asked Jacob what he would like to be paid. Jacob replied that he would work for Laban for seven years if he would allow him to marry Rachel. Laban agreed and Jacob began his seven years of work.

After the seven years had passed the arrangements for the wedding were made. However, once the ceremony was over Jacob realised to his horror that he had married Leah, Laban's elder daughter rather than Rachel, the one he loved.

When Jacob asked Laban why he had done this, Laban replied that it was not the custom to allow the younger daughter to marry first.

Jacob promised to work another seven years in return for being allowed to marry Rachel as well.

At this time it was quite normal for a man to have several wives.

TPD

Do you think that Jacob deserved to be treated in this way?

Why or why not?

TPD PD

In the Bible in Galatians 6:7 it says

"A man reaps what he sows."

What do you think this means?

Do you agree with this statement?

BC

Create a cartoon strip showing the things that happened to Jacob from when he left his family up until his marriage to Rachel.

Moses

BACKGROUND

Jacob had twelve sons, but Joseph was his favourite. His brothers were jealous of him and were angry when Jacob gave Joseph a special coat.

One day when the brothers were out in the fields with their sheep, they saw Joseph coming in the distance. They talked about killing him, but the eldest brother saved Joseph by suggesting that they drop him into a dried up well. They did this and planned to tell their father that a wild animal had eaten him.

Just then, some merchants passed by on their way to Egypt and the brothers decided to sell Joseph to them.

In Egypt, they sold Joseph as a slave, but he was very hard-working and was soon promoted.

Joseph had a very special gift – he was able to tell people what their dreams meant. **Pharaoh** had a dream about seven fat cows and seven thin cows. Joseph warned him that the dream meant there would be seven years of good crops in Egypt and seven years of famine.

Pharaoh believed that Joseph was a wise man and put him in charge of Egypt. During the seven years of good crops, Joseph stored up huge barns of grain. When the famine began, Joseph opened the barns and people from many countries came to buy food.

There was also a famine where Joseph's brothers lived, so they decided to go to Egypt to get food. His brothers did not recognise Joseph but he knew them immediately. In the end Joseph forgave them and brought them to live in Egypt.

Jacob had been given a new name: Israel. All his sons, and all their children and aunts and uncles became known as the 'children of Israel', or sometimes 'Israelites'.

The years went by and the number of Israelites in Egypt grew. The new Pharaoh noticed how strong they were becoming and he was worried that they would turn against him. So the Egyptians made the Israelites slaves and put taskmasters in charge of them. They were made to build cities and great buildings and do all kinds of hard work.

The Israelites were still growing in number so the Pharaoh did a very cruel thing. He ordered that every Israelite boy born should be thrown into the River Nile. Only one was saved. His name was **Moses**.

TPD

Why do you think Pharaoh killed all the Israelite boys?

THE BIRTH OF MOSES

TPD
Cit
PD

1 How do people react when a new baby is born into a family?
2 What sort of preparations do they make?
3 How would they feel if someone tried to harm their baby?

After he was born, Moses' mother hid him for three months until he became too big to hide. She made a basket out of reeds and coated it with tar to keep the water out. She put Moses inside the basket and hid it in the rushes at the edge of the River Nile. His sister Miriam stayed close by to keep watch.

Soon the Pharaoh's daughter, a princess, came to the river to bathe and she saw the basket. Inside she found the baby and guessed that he was an Israelite child. She decided to save him, and took him back to the palace to be brought up as her own son. Miriam asked the princess if she would go and find a Israelite nanny to look after the child. The princess agreed and Miriam went and got her own mother to care for Moses.

The princess called the baby Moses because it means 'drawn out of the water'.

MI

1 What was Pharaoh afraid of?

2 Why did Moses' mother hide him?

3 How did Moses' mother hide him?

4 Who found the basket and what did she decide to do?

BC

Draw a picture of the basket being found.

Include speech bubbles in your drawing, and fill in what each person is saying.

BC
WO

Role-play

Write a drama about Moses being found amongst the rushes. What characters will you need?

The people acting are not allowed to write the script. Choose a director of the play and arrange rehearsals with the actors.

Remember that you could put in characters that the Bible doesn't mention.

Moses grew up as an Egyptian prince but in his heart he knew he was a Israelite – perhaps his mother had told him.

One day many years later, when Moses was a man, he went out to watch the people at work. He saw one of the Egyptian **taskmasters** beating an Israelite slave. He was very angry and hit the taskmaster, killing him. He dug a shallow grave in the sand and buried the body.

The next day Moses saw two Israelite men fighting and he went to separate them. Moses asked, "Why are you hitting your friend?" One of the men turned angrily to Moses and shouted, "Are you going to kill me as you killed the Egyptian yesterday?" Moses knew that his terrible crime had been discovered.

He panicked as he thought about what might happen to him if the Pharaoh found out what he had done. He decided to run away from Egypt and go to a place called **Midian**.

ICT
MI
BC

You are the editor of the *Daily Israeli*, a newspaper for Israelites living in Egypt. Choose one of the articles below:

Design and write a front page article about the events surrounding the birth of Moses and the murder of the Israeli boys.

OR

Design and write a front cover article about the events surrounding the mysterious death of an Egyptian taskmaster and the sudden disappearance of the Egyptian prince Moses.

For either article, include a catchy headline, interviews with eyewitnesses, pictures of the events, and anything else you think would make your report interesting. Wordprocess it if you can.

ACCEPTING A CALL

Are you ever asked to do things that you don't want to do? Of course! This happens to everybody sometimes. But the important thing to think about is, how do you react when this happens to you?

Christians believe that God also calls people to do a particular job, eg to become a missionary, minister, nun or doctor. People call this a **vocation**.

Com
TPD
PD

Look at the pictures below. These are some of the ways Christians today say they have heard God calling them.

In dreams

Using other people

By phone

From the Bible

By post

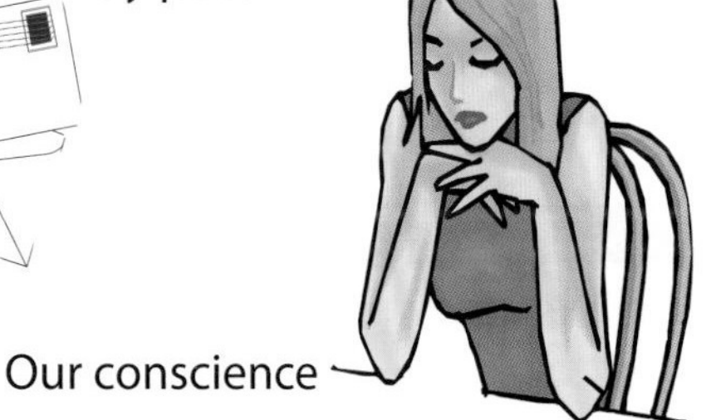

Our conscience

Talk about each one and think up some possible situations where these methods could be used.

It is not always easy to do what others ask us to do, especially if it is not what we *want* to do.

Sometimes we may ignore the request or we may get cross and suggest that someone else does it.

This was what happened to Moses when God called him to go back to Egypt.

THE BURNING BUSH

When Moses ran away from Egypt he went to Midian.

He stopped to rest at a well and seven girls came along to water their father's sheep. When they had drawn the water, some shepherds came along to chase them away and take the water for their own animals. Moses helped the girls who then told their father Jethro. Jethro invited Moses to stay with him. Eventually Moses married one of his daughters, Zipporah.

Everything was going well for Moses. He had a wife and family. Then one day something took place that would change his life again.

Moses was out with the sheep when he saw a strange sight. It was a bush that seemed to be on fire, but did not burn away.

He went nearer to see what it was. Then he heard a voice speaking to him.

You can read about this in Exodus 3:1-21.

TPD
PD

Moses heard a voice coming from a bush. It's not everyday that you hear a bush talking to you!

How do you think you would have reacted if this happened to you?

This would have been just as strange for Moses as it would be for us today.

The voice that spoke to Moses was God's and he said:

Take off your shoes; you are standing on holy ground.

Go back to Egypt and free my people.

Moses was very afraid – he did not want to go back to Egypt. Moses began to make excuses, saying:

- I am a nobody.
- Who will I say sent me?
- Suppose they don't believe me?
- I am a poor speaker.
- Send someone else!

God tried to prove to Moses that he would be with him by performing two miracles.

God told Moses to throw down his wooden staff. It became a snake! When he lifted it up it became a wooden staff again.

God told Moses to put his hand inside his coat. When he took it out it was covered in the signs of **leprosy**. He was told to put his hand inside his coat again and when he took it out the leprosy had gone.

Moses still insisted that he could not speak well so God said Aaron, Moses' brother, could go with him. Aaron was a good speaker, so his job would be to speak for Moses.

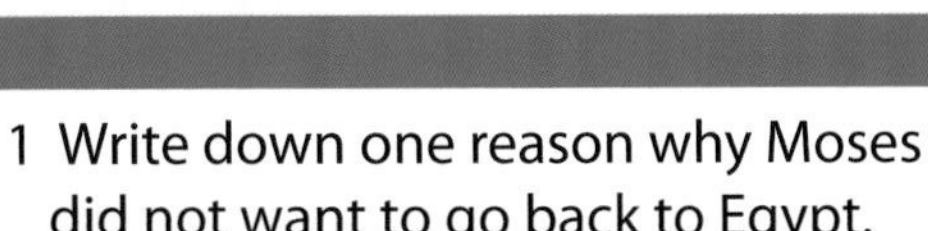

MI

1 Write down one reason why Moses did not want to go back to Egypt.

2 Write down two of the excuses Moses made.

3 Who went to Egypt with Moses?

4 How did God try to prove to Moses that he really was God and that he would support Moses in what he was asking him to do?

MI
TPD

The burning bush is the symbol of a particular Christian denomination. Which one is it?

Why do you think this symbol was chosen?

THE TEN PLAGUES

When Moses and Aaron came to Pharaoh and asked him to free the Israelites, he refused. He did not want to lose his slaves. So God sent ten **plagues**.

MI

Look up Exodus chapters 7-11.

Write down what the ten plagues were.

Each time a plague came, Pharaoh agreed to let the people go, but as soon as the plague had gone he changed his mind.

The last plague was the worst. The first-born male in every household throughout Egypt, even the first-born animals, was killed.

Even Pharaoh's eldest son died during this plague.

The Israelites were kept safe because God told them to mark the door posts of their houses with the blood of a lamb. If they did this, the plague of death would pass them by. Jews still remember this important event during the **Passover** festival.

After plague number ten the Pharaoh agreed to let the slaves go.

MI

Read Exodus chapter 12:1-14 and 21-28 to discover the instructions God gave the Israelites.

Read verse 5 and write down the three things mentioned about the lamb they were to choose.

TPD

Why do you think the chosen lamb had to be perfect?

THE PASSOVER MEAL

Before leaving Egypt the Israelites had time for a quick meal, but they had to hurry before the Pharaoh changed his mind.

Read Exodus chapter 12:8-11 to find out the things they ate and how they were to be eaten.

MI BC WO Cit

Find out how Jews celebrate the Passover today.

Make a classroom display.

THE EXODUS

Moses led the Israelites out of Egypt as quickly as possible. This event is called the **Exodus**.

TPD

Do you think this is a good name?

Why or why not?

God stayed with his people and guided them on their journey.

Read Exodus 13:21 to discover how God guided the Israelites.

BC

Copy out the sentences, filling in the blanks and illustrating each one with a drawing.

During the day they were guided by a _________________ .

At night they were guided by a _______ .

Moses led the people south toward **Mount Sinai** before moving north again, towards **Canaan** – the Promised Land.

It would have been much quicker to walk across the desert straight to Canaan.

TPD

Why might Moses have led the people away from Canaan first?

When the Israelites had gone Pharaoh was sorry, as he had lost all his slaves. He took more than six hundred chariots and many horsemen and soldiers and went after them.

You can imagine how afraid the Israelites were when they saw the Egyptians coming after them. There was no escape – the Pharaoh was behind them and the sea was in front of them.

The Israelites cried out to God. God told Moses to hold his rod out over the sea. Moses obeyed and an east wind drove back the water until the people could go safely across.

The Egyptian army followed but the water began to flow back. The wheels of their chariots became stuck in the wet sand and they all drowned.

TPD

1 What do you think this incident taught the Israelites about God?

2 Write down two words that you feel sum up Moses' faith at this time.

MI BC

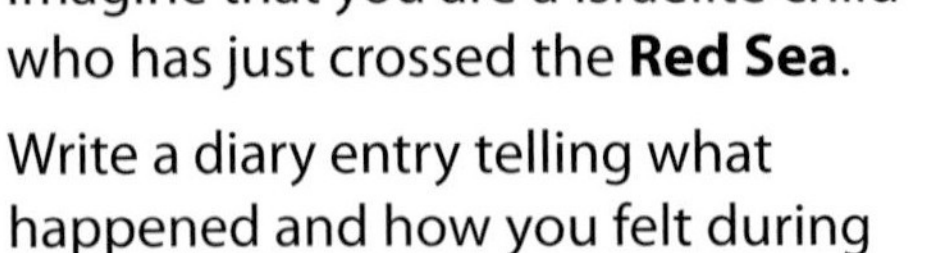

Imagine that you are a Israelite child who has just crossed the **Red Sea**.

Write a diary entry telling what happened and how you felt during the crossing.

MI BC Cit

Find a map of Egypt and Israel. Make a sketch drawing of it.

Mark on it:

- The Red Sea
- Mount Sinai
- Jerusalem
- The Dead Sea

BC

Draw a picture of the crossing of the Red Sea.

Role-play

Moses: (*enters and crosses to podium*) Good morning, my name is Moses, the adopted son of Pharaoh's daughter. This will be my last press conference with the Egyptian press before I lead my people across the Red Sea. As I have said repeatedly in previous press conferences, all of the misery that the people of Egypt have suffered during the ten plagues could have been avoided if Pharaoh, King of Egypt, had merely let my people go when I first requested it.

Reporter 1: Moses, are you aware that Pharaoh has mobilised his army and is on his way here to wipe out your people?

Moses: I am aware of that. That's why I called this press conference. I wanted to put this attack into perspective for both Egyptians and Israelites.

Reporter 2: You don't seem to be very nervous, for a man who is about to be killed by Pharaoh.

Moses: That's my point in calling this press conference. There is not the remotest chance that my people will receive even the slightest injury at the hands of the Egyptian army.

Reporter 2: How can you say that?! The Egyptian army is the most powerful and feared army in the whole world!

Moses: I am aware of that. I am also aware of who the army opposes when they attack us.

Reporter 2: You must be joking!

Reporter 3: I have seen false pride before but this takes the prize.

Reporter 4: Moses, are you aware that your people don't have a single sword or spear among them? Are you expecting the Israelites to fend off an attack of swords and arrows with bare fists?!

Moses: That's not what I'm saying at all. I would have thought that after ten plagues, the message to Pharaoh and the Egyptians would be clear by now.

Reporter 5: What message have we missed?

Moses: Over four hundred years ago, the God who created the universe out of nothing promised our ancestor Abraham that the Israelites were his special people. He promised that anyone who helped them would be blessed by God and anyone who harmed them would be punished by God. Didn't the ten plagues teach you ANYTHING?!

Reporter 5: Are you saying that your god, this god of your ancestor Abraham, will somehow protect you against the most powerful army in the world?

Moses: That's exactly what I'm saying. I'm saying that if Pharaoh doesn't call off this attack he will experience the **eleventh** plague.

Reporter 6: Can you be more specific? What will be the nature of this eleventh plague?

Moses: I'm not sure. God rarely reveals his plans in great detail, because his plans are usually more than man can imagine.

Reporter 6: Can you at least give us a clue?

Moses: The only message I have received from the Lord God is a message to our people. It is the reason I called this press conference. The message from God is "**Stand firm**".

Reporter 7: "Stand firm"? That's it?! "Stand firm"?

Moses: Stand firm. We Israelites seem to have a very short memory. We just witnessed the most impressive show of God's power since creation. But as soon as my people heard rumours that the army was on the way, they forgot about how God protected them from all ten plagues back in Egypt and how God has promised to protect them in the future. They forgot and they began to fear for their lives. God says, "Stand firm."

Reporter 7: What could your god do to protect your people from the world's most powerful army?

Moses: It's quite possible that the eleventh plague will kill Pharaoh himself and wipe out his entire army.

Reporter 8: But the Egyptian army has your people trapped with your backs to the Red Sea. It will take you months to transport your people across in rowing boats, but the army will be here tomorrow! Your people are like sitting ducks!

Moses: All I know is that God promised Abraham that he would protect his people. And he has kept his promise so far. Our people have grown in numbers under God's protection in Egypt. And now I'm confident that God will protect us as we cross over the sea tomorrow.

Reporter 8: The only question is *how*?

Moses: I'm sure God will make it clear to all tomorrow before the Egyptian army arrives. Who knows? Perhaps the God who turned the River Nile into blood will part the waters of the Red Sea and let us *walk* across on dry land.

Reporter 9: Even if your pie-in-the-sky *walk* to the Promised Land becomes a reality, I don't see how that will protect you from the Egyptian army. Remember, they have chariots. You are on foot! They could follow you *through* the Red Sea.

Moses: Let's suppose, for the sake of argument that God chooses to part the waters of the Red Sea and let us walk on dry land through it. As soon as the last Israelite gets to the other side, what's to keep God from reversing the flow of water and drowning the entire Egyptian army in one fell swoop? What I'm saying is, if we don't panic, if we stand firm and trust God to do what he promised he would do, we Israelites will be protected from the Egyptian army as surely as we were protected from the ten plagues.

(shouts) STAND FIRM!

(exits)

©2005 Bob Snook
http://www.fea.net/bobsnook
e-mail: bobsnook@fea.net

THE DIFFICULT JOURNEY

The Israelites had a wonderful experience of God at the beginning of their journey. They had proved that they had a God who would not leave them in difficult times.

The Book of Exodus tells us about three problems that the Israelites faced on their journey.

MI

Copy out and complete the tables below to discover what the problems were and how they dealt with them.

You will find out if they really learned to depend on God.

PROBLEM 1

Cause of the problem	**Exodus 16:1-3** They had no ____.
What did they do?	**Exodus 16:2** The people ____.
Solution to the problem	**Exodus 16:4-21** God sent down ____ in the evening and _____ in the morning.

PROBLEM 2

Cause of the problem	**Exodus 17:1** They had no ____.
What did they do?	**Exodus 17:2-3** The people ____.
Solution to the problem	**Exodus 17:4-6** God told Moses to strike the _________ with his _________. When he did this _________ came out of the rock.

PROBLEM 3

Cause of the problem	**Exodus 17:8** The ____ came and attacked the Israelites.
What did they do?	**Exodus 17:9-10** They went out to fight the Amalekites and ____ was put in charge of the fighting. Moses went up on a ____ holding the stick ____ had instructed him to carry. ____and Hur went with Moses.
Solution to the problem	**Exodus 17:11-13** When Moses held his arms up the ____ won, but when he put his arms down the ____ started winning. Aaron and ____ helped to hold his arms up when they got tired. The Israelites _____ the Amalekites.

The Israelites' reaction to these problems was to grumble and complain. This was not just against Moses, but they were also doubting God's presence and power to help them.

MI

1 When the Israelites were faced with problems they (opanclmide). Unscramble the letters.

2 Read Exodus 17:7. Write out the sentence which shows how the Israelites questioned God.

GOD'S RULES

Com
TPD
Cit
PD

Discuss why rules are necessary in the following situations:

Rules are really standards which control how we behave. If we had no rules the whole country would be in a mess.

We need rules to control our behaviour and to encourage respect for other people and their property.

Rules are also needed for the safety and protection of other people and ourselves.

The Ten Commandments

God gave Moses a set of ten rules which are still important to many people.

About three months after they left Egypt, the Israelites came to Mount Sinai. They camped at the foot of the mountain.

Moses went up the mountain and God gave him ***Ten Commandments***.

Read them in Exodus 20:1-17.

The first four commandments are to do with God's followers' duty towards him. The last six are about their duty towards each other.

When Moses came down the mountain he heard singing and shouting. He had been away for forty days and the Israelites did not know what had become of him. They thought he was not coming back.

The people had grown afraid and had persuaded Aaron make an idol for them to worship. Aaron knew this was wrong but he wanted to please the people. He melted down their gold jewellery and made a golden calf, which the Israelites started to worship.

When Moses saw this he was very angry and threw down the commandment tablets, breaking them. He smashed the calf into small pieces and warned the people never to do such a thing again.

Duty to God

1 Worship no God but me.
2 Don't worship idols.
3 Don't use my name wrongly.
4 Keep the Sabbath day holy.

Duty to man

5 Respect your father and mother.
6 Do not murder.
7 Do not commit adultery.
8 Do not steal.
9 Do not accuse anyone falsely.
10 Do not envy others.

MI

Find out if there have ever been any films made or books written about Moses and the Ten Commandments.

Have you seen or read any?

TPD

List five things that people sometimes think are more important than God.

3 Do not use my name wrongly.

TPD

How is this commandment broken today?

Christians believe that they should not use God's name as a swear word or break promises made in his name.

Are the Ten Commandments still needed today?

Christians say the Ten Commandments apply to them too, even after thousands of years.

1 Worship no God but me.

2 Don't worship idols.

You might think that these are two easy commandments to keep.

Christians are instructed not to worship false gods, idols, or Satan.

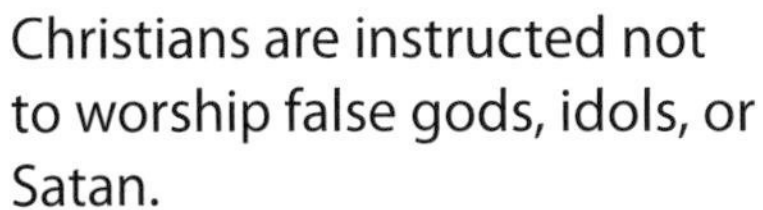

But people can have false gods without even realising it. Some people trust things like money or a job to make them happy. So, if a Christian loves something more than God, they are not putting him first. This breaks the first commandment.

4 Keep the Sabbath day holy.

MI
TPD
PD

Find out what day of the week is the Sabbath.

Why do Christians have their special day of rest on Sunday?

Christians believe that God introduced the Sabbath so that people would have a day of rest.

In what ways might a day of rest be good for people?

This commandment says we should have one special day, not just for religious reasons, but also for rest and family time.

If we work for seven days a week, we end up tired and irritable. Therefore, one day of rest is for our own good.

TPD

Some people do have to work on a Sunday.

How many can you think of?

Com TPD WO Cit

Organise a class debate on the motion that:

"No businesses or leisure facilities should be open on Sunday".

5 Respect your father and mother.

MI TPD SM PD

Look up the word 'respect' in a dictionary.

In what ways can we show respect to our parents?

Discuss why is it sometimes difficult to obey this command.

6 Do not murder.

This one seems very simple. Killing another person is wrong. But is it as simple as that?

TPD Cit PD

A soldier who goes to war in the name of his country will probably have to kill someone.

Is this soldier guilty of murder?

7 Do not commit adultery.

Adultery is when a person who is married has a relationship with someone else.

TPD Cit PD

If a husband or wife is unfaithful, what consequences can this have on the family?

8 Do not steal.

TPD SM Cit PD

Write down what you think the word 'steal' means.

Many of us think of stealing as something like robbing a bank, housebreaking, stealing from a shop, and so on. But stealing can be other things too.

Do you think what takes place in the following three examples could be called 'stealing'?

If so, who is the money being stolen from?

1 A customer finds a roll of banknotes lying on the floor of a bank, puts the money in his pocket and tells no-one.

2 Someone earns money from a business but deliberately does not pay the right amount of tax.

3 You are given too much change at a supermarket check-out. You notice this at once but you do not give it back.

TPD PD

Is it ever acceptable to steal?

Have a class discussion about three situations when you think stealing might be necessary.

9 Do not accuse anyone falsely.

This really means, 'Do not tell lies'.

The people you lie to may not know, but Christians believe that God knows.

TPD
PD

Write down two reasons why someone might tell a lie.

Can telling lies be bad for the person telling them?

The Boy who cried Wolf

There once was a shepherd boy who was bored as he sat on the hillside watching the village sheep.

To amuse himself he took a great breath and shouted, "Wolf! Wolf! The Wolf is chasing the sheep! "The villagers came running up the hill to help the boy drive the wolf away. But when they arrived at the top of the hill, they found no wolf. The boy laughed at the sight of their angry faces. "Don't cry 'wolf', shepherd boy," said the villagers, "when there's no wolf!" They went back down the hill, grumbling.

Later, the boy shouted again, "Wolf! Wolf! The wolf is chasing the sheep!" To his delight, he watched the villagers run up the hill to help him drive the wolf away. When the villagers saw no wolf they sternly said, "Save your frightened song for when there is really something wrong! Don't cry 'wolf' when there is NO wolf!" But the boy just grinned and watched them go grumbling down the hill once more.

Later, he saw a *real* wolf prowling about his flock. Alarmed, he leaped to his feet and shouted as loudly as he could, "Wolf! Wolf!" But the villagers thought he was trying to fool them again, and so they didn't come.

At sunset, everyone wondered why the shepherd boy hadn't returned to the village with the sheep. They went up the hill to find the boy. They found him weeping. "There really was a wolf here! The flock has scattered! I cried out, 'Wolf!' Why didn't you come?"

An old man tried to comfort the boy as they walked back to the village. "We'll help you look for the lost sheep in the morning," he said, putting his arm around the youth, ***"Nobody believes a liar ... even when he is telling the truth!"***

TPD
PD

Is there any difference between a white lie and a black lie?

Have a debate in class on the motion that:

'It is sometimes right to tell lies'.

10 Do not envy.

ICT
TPD
PD

Look up the words 'envy' and 'covet' in the dictionary or internet.

Christians believe that they must not be envious of what others have.

If someone covets what others have, how might it affect that person?

BC
TPD
WO
PD

Draw out a table like the one below.

Pick which of the commandments you think are relevant today and which are not.

Discuss your decision with the rest of your class.

The commandments which apply today	The commandments which do not apply today

Write down reasons why some people think the commandments are still important today.

Write down reasons why some people think the commandments are no longer important.

Make up ten ***'teen commandments'*** that could help teenagers live their lives in the 21st century.

Ruth

In this unit you are going to find out about a famous Old Testament woman called Ruth. Before you do this we need think about ourselves. Let's be selfish for a moment!

Think about your class. You are all nearly the same age and go to the same school. But you are individuals. You are all different.

ATTITUDES TO WOMEN

TPD SM WO

Together with a partner, share some ideas about 'differences' and then copy and complete the diagram below:

Me | *My friend*

Differences | Similarities | Differences

TPD EfE PD

Anything you can do I can do better!

Are we guilty of **stereotyping**?

Read these statements:

Blondes are stupid.
Girls work harder at secondary school than boys.
Women make better nurses than men.
Women are worse drivers than men.
Men do better at sports than women.
Men are useless in the kitchen.
DIY is a man's job.
Men are more violent than women.
Tall men are more successful than short men.

Part A

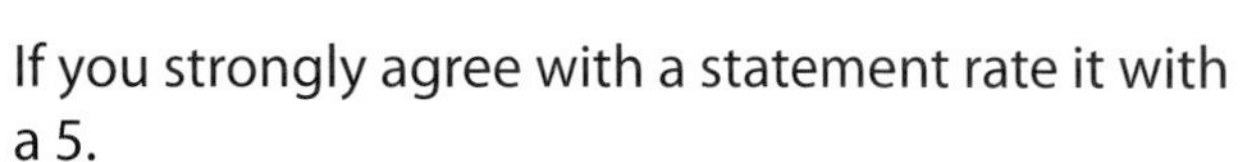

If you strongly agree with a statement rate it with a 5.

If you agree with a statement rate it with a 4.

If you don't feel strongly one way or the other rate it with a 3.

If you disagree with a statement rate it with a 2.

If you strongly disagree with a statement rate it with a 1.

Part B

Compare your answers with someone else. Is your scoring the same?

What about the responses of the rest of the class?

Part C

Using the responses of the class draw up a pie chart or a bar graph to show the results.

MI TPD EfE PD

Although women have achieved equality in many things, there is still a range of different beliefs, practices and traditions associated with the different roles of men and women.

Can you think any such different beliefs, practices or traditions?

To get you started, think of religious traditions. Are there differences in the roles of men and women between churches? You might have to do some research on this.

TPD Cit PD

What influences your attitude to the other sex?

Is it your families? The media? Religious institutions eg churches? Your peers?

TPD EfE PD

Draw two overlapping circles.

Label one circle 'man' and the other 'woman'.

Put into the circles anything men and women do.

Where the circles overlap, write in anything that you think both do.

STEREOTYPING

TPD Cit

Do you think it would be wrong for people to stereotype you and your friends as if you all believed in the one thing or behaved in the same way?

Why or why not?

MI TPD WO PD

Male/female stereotyping – is there any truth in it?

Now that you have explored attitudes towards stereotyping we want you to think about your choices. Are there big differences between what boys and girls have said?

Copy out the table below and fill it in with your favourites. Put a first, second and third choice.

TV programme			
Film			
Music			
Food			
Sport			
Activity			

Now discuss these with the rest of your class. Is there any stereotyping? Have all the girls gone for the same kinds of choices?

RUTH – AN INSPIRATIONAL WOMAN

In Old Testament times, women had a different life to what they have today. The eldest man was responsible for making the decisions and did not have to consult his wife. Men could divorce their wives easily. Only men were allowed to own property. Women were expected to obey their husbands at all times.

Who was Ruth?

The period in which the events recorded in the book of Ruth happened are among the worst in Israel's history.

Find the book of Ruth in the Bible.

A famine forced Elimelech and his wife Naomi to leave their home in Bethlehem and go to the country of Moab, on the eastern shore of the Dead Sea.

Elimelech died and Naomi was left with her two sons Mahlon and Kilion, who marry two Moabite girls, Orpah and Ruth. Ten years later, Mahlon and Kilion also died.

MI

Draw Ruth's the family tree using the information you just read.

Naomi means 'someone who has found favour with God' or 'pleasant.'

Elimelech means 'My God is King'.

Ruth means 'compassion' or 'friend'.

ICT

Using an internet search engine, find out what your name means.

BC
TPD
Cit

How do you think Naomi and Elimelech might have felt when they left their home to go and search for food in Moab?

They were going to live in a strange land.

There are people today who have to leave their homes because of famine. Can you think of some reasons why?

Ruth Chapter 1: Decisions, decisions!

After the death of her sons, Naomi decided to return to Israel and she encouraged her daughters-in-law Ruth and Orpah to stay in Moab.

As a widow, under the law of the time, Naomi was to be provided for by the nearest relative of her dead husband but she had no relations in Moab.

Naomi had no other sons for Orpah and Ruth to marry. Orpah decided to stay in her homeland so that she might remarry. But Ruth was willing to give up this possibility so that she could care for Naomi.

Naomi changed her name to Mara, meaning 'bitter', to show the sadness she felt.

Her life had been very tough.

TPD
PD

Thought shower

What big decisions do you think you will have to make in the future?

Do you think Ruth was right in her big decision?

In her place, would you have done the same?

The Moabites

Among the Israelites, friendly relations with the Moabites were not encouraged and marrying one was forbidden.

It is said the Moabites were not allowed to worship at the Tabernacle, because they had not let the Israelites pass through their land as they left Egypt.

Orpah and Ruth were Moabite girls so Naomi's sons had married 'foreigners'.

MI

1 Why did Elimelech and his family leave Bethlehem?
2 Where did they move to?
3 What great loss did Naomi suffer?
4 Why did Naomi decide to return to Bethlehem?
5 Who went with Naomi when she left?
6 What did Naomi tell her daughters-in-law to do?
7 In verses 1:20 and 21 what did Naomi say God has been doing in her life?
8 Write out the key verse – verse 1:16

Ruth Chapter 2

There were not many ways for a widow to make a living in Israel. One way was to **glean** the fields. Naomi and Ruth arrived in Bethlehem at the start of the barley harvest.

When the wheat and barley were ready to be harvested, people were employed to cut it and tie it into bundles. Any barley stalks that were dropped were to be left for poor people who picked it up. This was called gleaning. This way poor people got some food free.

Now it was Ruth who was in a foreign land among strangers. Instead of depending on someone to look after her, she decided to take action and went to glean in the fields.

The owner of the fields was Boaz and he was a relative of Naomi's dead husband.

He noticed Ruth working in his fields and asked who she was. Boaz was concerned for Ruth when he was told that she was a member of his extended family.

He was a kind man and allowed any poor person to glean in his fields. He made special provisions for Ruth and told his workers to let grain fall in her path.

Boaz advised Ruth to stay with his servants until the harvest was over.

Naomi must have been astonished at the amount of grain that Ruth had brought home. She guessed that Ruth had been working for a generous landowner, and she praised the man for his generosity, whoever he was.

Then, Ruth told Naomi that she had worked in Boaz's field. At this news, Naomi praised God, and had an idea.

We have already learnt that if a woman lost her husband the law said that the nearest male relative was to care for her. Ruth had no such relative in Israel.

But, there were **Kinsmen Redeemers**. Kinsmen Redeemers had a special role. Their name means to receive, redeem or buy back. The Law of Moses contained ways to help poor people and the Kinsmen Redeemers were part of this. For example, if a poor person had to sell land the Kinsman Redeemer could step in a buy it back. He was the nearest of 'kin'. They were usually very rich people. If a person had been forced into slavery the Kinsman Redeemer could buy their freedom or, if a man died, the Kinsman Redeemer could marry his widow.

Naomi told Ruth to observe the customs so that Boaz would know that he could be her Kinsman Redeemer. He could either marry her or find someone else who would marry her.

So Ruth observed the customs and made a discovery. Boaz had been thinking about marrying her! But there is a complication. There is a male relative nearer to the family than Boaz.

When Ruth returns to Naomi she tells her that Boaz will carry through his promise. He must have a reputation for keeping his word. Look up Ruth 3:13.

Ruth Chapter 3

TPD SM EfE PD

Planning

Everyone can set themselves goals.

What goal could you set yourself? Would it be to eat more healthily or improve your exam results?

What steps could you take to achieve your goal?

Think of a goal and come up with five steps to help you achieve that goal.

MI TPD

Character study: Boaz

From chapters 1-3 select **four** pieces of information about Boaz and explain what they show about him.

TPD PD

Boaz the hero

Boaz was going to take Ruth from a life of hardship. Name some people you think are modern day heroes.

What makes a hero?

Is it someone who scores a winning goal?

Is it someone who rescues people from a fire?

Ruth Chapter 4 – The happy ending

Boaz went to see the nearest male relative.

There is property in Naomi's family. As the nearest male relative, this man had the right to buy it. He decided he would.

But then he found out that if he bought the property then he would have to marry the widow Ruth. When he discovered this, the man changed his mind so the way was clear for Boaz to marry Ruth.

MI
TPD

Character study: Ruth

What sort of person was Ruth?

Use the words in the box below to write some sentences about her.

gracious	sad	hard-working
angry	poor	loving
brave	jealous	kind
beautiful	distressed	tragic
happy	humble	patient
strong	rich	

ICT
BC
WO

Drama

In groups, choose one of the scenes from the book of Ruth and write a short drama based on it.

INSPIRATIONAL WOMEN

MI
BC
TPD
PD

Look up the word inspirational. Do you think Ruth was an inspirational woman? Why or why not?

Can you think of any inspirational women today?

Maybe you have a female relative who has inspired you.

If so, write a paragraph her and how she has influenced you.

Look through newspapers and magazines for pictures of women you think are inspirational. Bring them in to class and choose some to have a discussion about.

Inspirational women in history

Emmeline Pankhurst (1858–1928)

Emmeline Pankhurst led the movement for the right of women in Britain to vote in elections.

She was born in 1858 in Manchester. She married Richard Pankhurst in 1879. He was a lawyer.

In 1889 Emmeline founded the Women's Franchise League, which fought to allow married women to vote in local elections.

In October 1903 she helped found the more **militant** Women's Social and Political Union (WSPU). This organisation became known for its militant activities and its members were the first to be called '**suffragettes**'.

Emmeline Pankhurst being arrested in 1914

After receiving a £2,000 grant from the government, the WSPU organised a demonstration in London. Members carried banners with slogans. There were 30,000 people at the meeting. Emmeline Pankhurst called on **trades unions** to let women work in those industries that had mostly men up to now. Emmeline's daughters, Christabel and Sylvia, both supported their mother. As a suffragette, Emmeline was arrested many times and even went on hunger strike.

The suffragettes' campaign eventually contributed to many women getting the vote. In 1918 an Act of Parliament was passed giving women over 30 years old (or over 21 if they were householders or were married to householders) the right to vote.

Emmeline died on 14 June 1928.

BC WO

Divide the class into small groups.

Imagine that you are producing a short film about the life of Emmeline Pankhurst. Decide on a scene that you would like to include, eg Emmeline's speech at the WSPU demonstration.

Think about the following:

Characters

Setting

Action

Draw up a plan in your notebook and then rehearse your scene. You might be asked to act it out for the rest of the class!

JESUS AND WOMEN

At the time of Jesus, Jewish men thanked God daily in their prayers that they had not been born a woman. Men and women worshipped in separate areas in the Temple and synagogues.

Jesus was not like other men of his time and treated men and women the same. There are several stories in the Gospels where Jesus showed that women were equal to men.

Some Christians today believe that men and women should have equality. Other Christians believe that men are meant to be leaders and women should support their husbands.

WOMEN IN THE CHURCH TODAY

The Catholic Church does not believe that women should be ordained as priests.

Other churches such as the Methodist, Presbyterian and Church of Ireland have women ministers. In 1976, Rev Ruth Patterson, a Presbyterian minister, was the first woman in Ireland to be ordained.

Com TPD WO PD

The four corners debate

The four corners of your classroom will represent the following viewpoints:

I agree

I do not agree

I am not sure

I would like to agree but...........

Now look at this statement: Women should be allowed to be ordained priests or ministers in the church.

Move to the corner which best describes your view.

Now one group must try to convince those in another a group why they should change their minds.

You can move once and *only once* if you change your mind after hearing what others have to say.

Don't move until your teacher says it is time!

At the end your teacher will record the number of pupils in each corner.

Did anyone change their mind? If so, why?

Com MI TPD Cit

Talk about what you think equality means.

Organise a class debate on the following:

"Women should have children or a career. They have to choose one or the other."

The Life of Jesus

The world of Jesus

Geography

Where is Israel in relation to the rest of the world?

If you look at the map you will see that Israel is a real country that still exists today. It is not just a fairy-tale place that existed in the Bible. Israel is a real country, with real people, a mix of different religions and many religious and political problems.

At the time of Jesus this region was called Palestine.

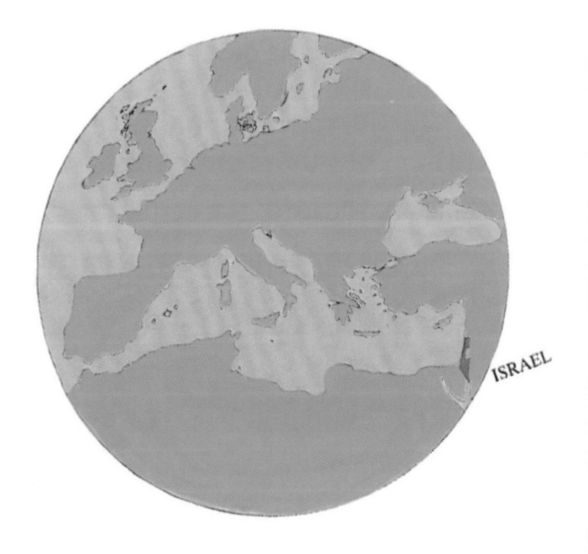

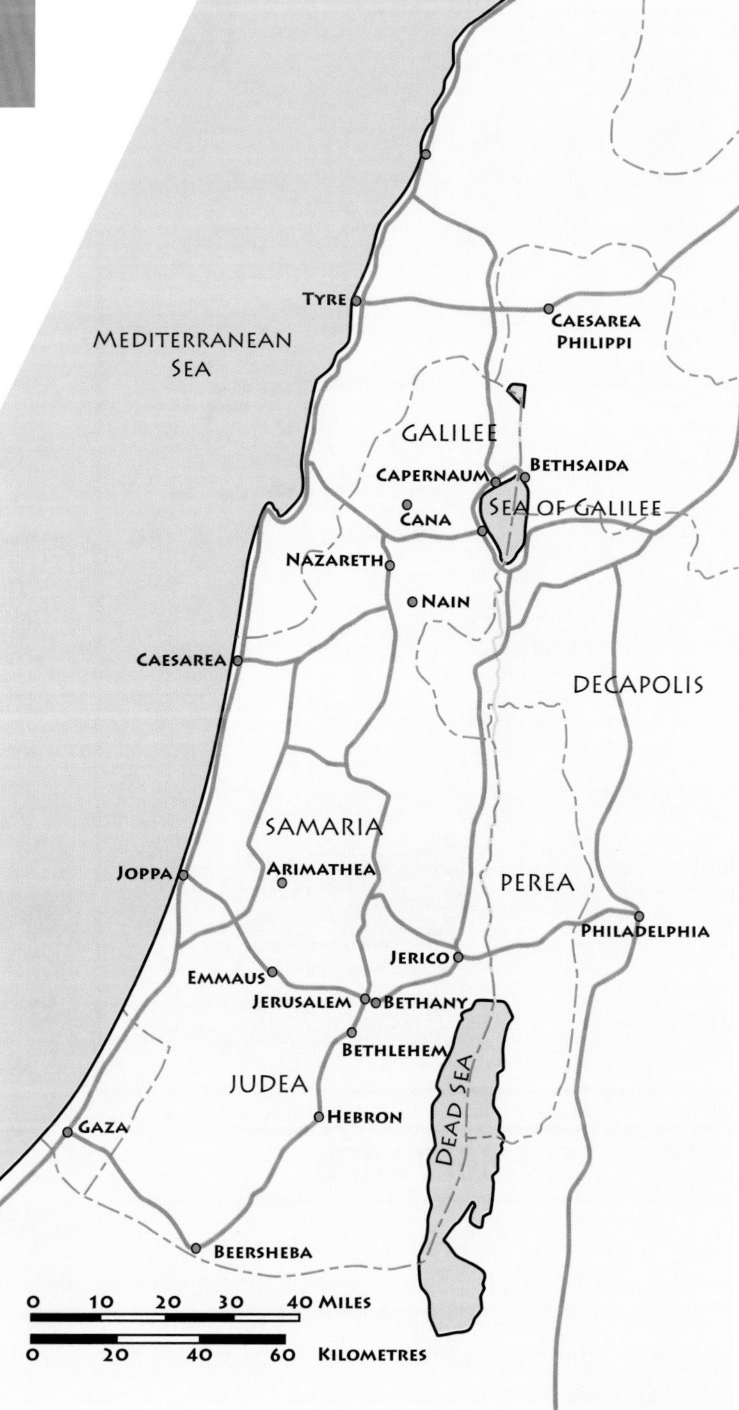

A map of Palestine at the time of Jesus.

The flag of Israel is white with a blue six pointed star and two blue horizontal stripes.

The star is the 'Star of David'. David was one of the most important kings in the history of Judaism.

The blue stripes on the flag are a reminder of the stripes on the Jewish prayer shawl.

MI
Cit

Look at the flags and find out what countries they belong to.

ISRAEL - THE HOLY LAND

The land where Jesus lived is called Israel today, but in the time of Jesus it was known as Palestine. It was a relatively small country, just a little bigger than Northern Ireland. It had three regions or provinces, called **Galilee**, **Samaria** and **Judea**.

Even though Palestine was a small country it was a very important one because of where it was. The continents of Europe, Asia and Africa meet at this point, meaning that a lot of people travelling had to pass through Palestine.

In 63BC, the Romans invaded and took control of Palestine, and they still ruled it when Jesus was alive. We will learn more about the Roman occupation later.

The north of Palestine was very different to the south. In the north was the province of Galilee with its lake called the **Sea of Galilee** (or Lake Galilee). It was on the shores of this sea that Jesus called the disciples and he calmed the storm on the Sea of Galilee. It is in the Jordan valley and was well known for its sudden storms and rough waters.

The land in Galilee was rich and fertile with both flat plains and steep hills. However as you moved south into Judea, the greenery was replaced by scorched desert. **Jerusalem**, the capital city, and **Bethlehem** the home town of Jesus, were in Judea.

The climate in Palestine was dry and hot, resulting in much of the land being parched. Palestine was bordered on the west by the **Mediterranean Sea** and on the east by the **River Jordan**.

The River Jordan ran from the north of the country, through the Sea of Galilee, down to the south and into the **Dead Sea**. Therefore it is not surprising that the name 'Jordan' means 'the river that rushes down'.

Part of Palestine was known as the Fertile Crescent.

The Dead Sea is in the region of Judea and is called this because the water is so salty that nothing can live in it.

MI
BC
Cit

Find out more about the Fertile Crescent. Make up a tourist leaflet describing the region.

The countryside of the land of Palestine

Com
MI
Cit

Imagine that you are describing Ireland to a person who has never visited the country. What would you say about it?

One of the highest temperatures ever recorded on earth, 53.8 degrees centigrade, was recorded in the Jordan valley.

Because of global warming and climate change, the Sea of Galilee has shrunk dramatically.

Jerusalem – the capital city

Many important events took place in or around Jerusalem.

One of the most characteristic features of the city was its walls. Jerusalem was entirely surrounded by walls as a defence against invaders.

The famous Old Testament king, David, made Jerusalem his capital, and it became the centre of the Jewish religion.

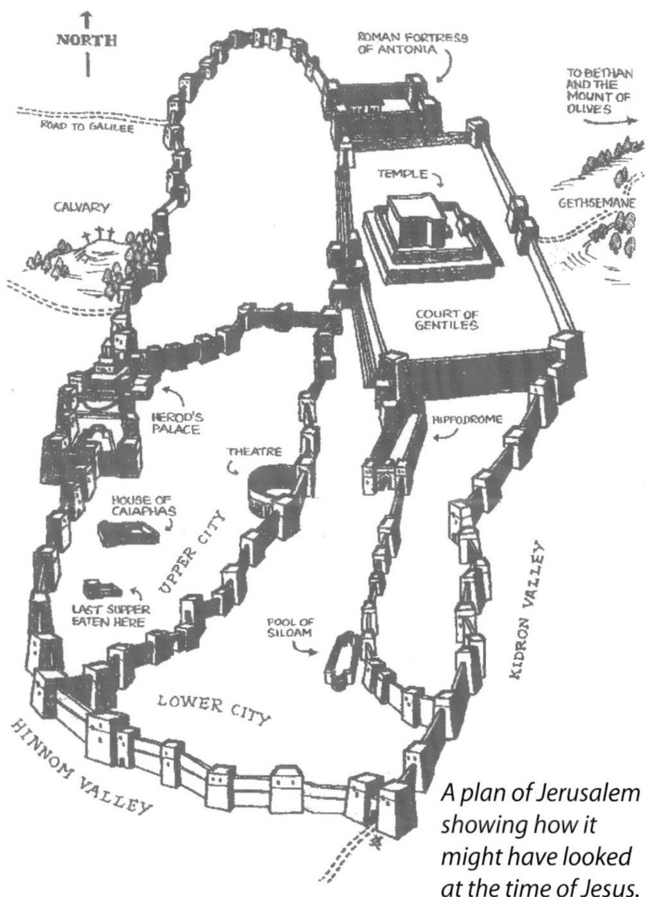

A plan of Jerusalem showing how it might have looked at the time of Jesus.

The Temple

The most important building in Jerusalem was the Temple.

In every town or village where there were more than ten men a synagogue was built. However, there was only one Temple in all of Palestine.

The first Temple was built by King Solomon in the 10th century BC. King Herod ordered the re-building of the Temple in 20BC.

It was huge and had different areas inside, eg the Court of the Women and the Court of the Gentiles.

The most holy part of the Temple was known as the **Holy of Holies**. This was a special room at the front of the Temple, which was separated off by a heavy embroidered curtain. The only person who was allowed to enter the Holy of Holies was the most important priest, known as the High Priest.

On the **Day of Atonement** (Yom Kippur) the High Priest offered up sacrifices on behalf of the people to **atone** for their sins.

The Temple was destroyed by the Romans in AD70 during a revolt by men strongly against the Romans. They were called **zealots**.

It was thought for many years that only one wall of the original Temple complex survived. This is called the **Western Wall** or the **Wailing Wall**. Many Jews pray at this wall.

However, in 2007, during excavations to lay pipes, further remains of the Temple were discovered.

The Wailing Wall

TPD

Read Luke 2:41-52.

What do you think of this story?

ICT

MI

BC

Do some research to find a floor plan of the Temple in Jerusalem.

Where could you look?

When you have found one, make your own drawing and label it.

MI

1 Who built the Temple in Jerusalem?
2 Why was the Holy of Holies such a special room?
3 Why was the Day of Atonement important for the Jews?
4 In what year did the Romans destroy the Temple?
5 Only one wall of the original Temple remains today. What is it called?

Com MI BC Cit

Imagine that you are a young person living in Palestine in Biblical times.

Write a letter to a pen pal in Northern Ireland describing the place where you live. Include details on the geography of Palestine, the climate, the Temple and anything else you think they might be interested to hear about.

History

THE ROMAN OCCUPATION OF THE LAND OF PALESTINE

In the year 63BC the Romans invaded the land of Palestine and took control.

The Jewish people did not like the presence of the Roman soldiers in their country.

How did the Romans control Palestine?

The Roman Empire was vast and many of the countries that the Romans invaded hated their presence. So the Romans had to control the people living in these countries. They did this through strict laws that were backed up by their well-trained and ruthless army.

Normally there were between 3000 to 5000 soldiers in a Roman **Legion** under the control of a **Legatus** (Legate).

A legion was broken down further into **Centuries**. Each Century had about 100 soldiers under the command of a **Centurion**.

Roman soldiers could be found in every town and village. It was their job to keep the peace, enforce Roman law, carry out punishments, control the roads and so on. A Roman soldier was well trained and disciplined.

MI

1 In what year did the Romans invade the land of Palestine?
2 The Romans had a vast Empire. What is an Empire?
3 Describe how the Roman army was organised.
4 Why were the Roman soldiers so important to the Roman Empire?

Roman law

Roman law and order was cruel and harsh. For example, a person found guilty of stealing, murder or rebellion against the Roman Empire would be crucified, which was a slow and painful way to die.

The Roman soldiers nailed the convicted criminal to a wooden cross. After a time they would break the victim's legs so that they could no longer support the body. The pressure of the body weight hanging on the arms forced the rib cage up, making it difficult for the person to breath so the person died from **asphyxiation**.

Many criminals were flogged with a whip called a **scourge.** This was made of leather straps with pieces of bone or metal embedded in them. This was used to whip Jesus before his crucifixion.

Stoning was a punishment set aside for women – often for committing adultery (ie being unfaithful to their husbands).

Ruthless penalties were also encouraged in Roman families and children were expected to obey their parents at all times. A son who attacked his father might be strangled or **garrotted**. An iron collar was put around his neck and tightened until he apologised.

TPD

Many Roman punishments were carried out in public.

Why do you think they did this?

TPD

PD

We have looked at Roman punishment as a harsh and cruel thing.

Do you think there was anything good about having such a disciplined and controlled system of punishment?

Explain your answer.

Was the Roman occupation of Palestine a good or a bad thing?

The Roman occupation of Palestine was a great blow to the pride of the Jewish people.

The Romans destroyed many of their sacred (holy) places. For example, they **defiled** the Temple and worshipped pagan gods. They broke many of the Jewish laws. For example, the Jewish respect for the Sabbath would not have been important to the Romans.

The Romans also imposed heavy taxes. This was a great burden to the people, many of whom were already very poor.

However, there were some good things about the Roman occupation. For example, the system of law and order brought peace to the country.

This Roman peace (known as *Pax Romana*), allowed business and trade to flourish, which was good for the economy of Palestine.

The Romans also started many building projects. They were responsible for things like building roads, public baths and **aqueducts**.

Herod the Great

Herod the Great was the ruler in Palestine when Jesus was born.

The Romans appointed him to rule over the Jews in 40BC. It is possible that they chose him because he was partly Jewish, but the Jews themselves didn't think he was.

During his lifetime Herod had ten wives and a large number of children. Many of them were put to death by his own orders.

TPD

Can you think of one cruel thing that Herod did during his lifetime?

If you can't, read Matthew chapter 2 to find out.

Although he was a cruel and much hated ruler, Herod did one good thing for the Jews during his lifetime. He was responsible for re-building the Temple in Jerusalem.

After his death his sons did not rule the country in a way that pleased the Romans, so they put a Roman governor or **Prefect** in charge of Judea. He was called **Pontius Pilate**.

MI

The Romans were **polytheistic**.

The Jews were **monotheistic**.

Find out what these words mean.

THE ZEALOTS

The Jews thought that the Messiah promised by God would be a military leader who would defeat the Romans. Jesus was not the type of Messiah that many people were hoping for.

Many of the Jewish people resented the Roman occupation of Palestine. They lived in constant hope that God would give them a leader who would free them.

One group in particular was prepared to resort to violence to remove the Romans from Palestine. They were known as the **Dagger Men** (**Sicarii**) or the **Zealots**.

They would not obey the Roman law and refused to pay their taxes. The Zealots were prepared to die for their faith. They were prepared to become **martyrs**.

They earned the name 'dagger men' because of the way they attacked Roman soldiers. A Zealot would go up to a Roman soldier, pull his dagger from his cloak, stab the soldier and disappear into the crowd.

The Romans reacted angrily towards the Zealots. The conflict between the Romans and the Zealots was the cause of the destruction of Jerusalem and the Temple in AD70.

Com MI BC WO

In groups, plan a presentation about the Zealots. Use these headings.

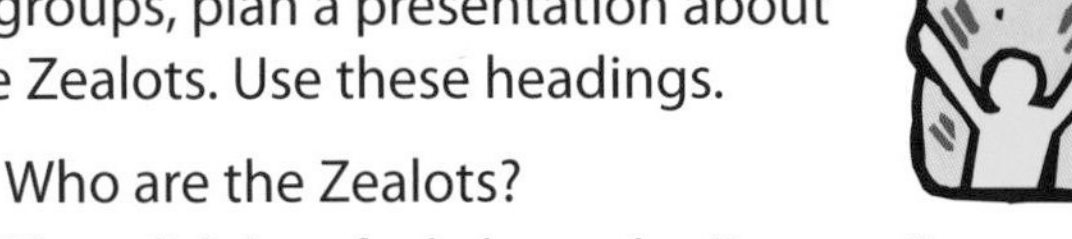

- Who are the Zealots?
- How did they feel about the Romans?
- How did they fight the Romans?
- What did the Romans do?

You could try to research more information if you like.

MI BC TPD Cit

Are there places today where people are living under rulers who are bad to them?

If so, find out about one of these places and make a collage of information about it.

TAKING IT FURTHER – JESUS HEALS A ROMAN CENTURION'S SERVANT

As we have seen, many of the Jews in Palestine hated the Romans.

They showed a great deal of prejudice and intolerance towards them. Many people would have expected Jesus, a Jew, to think about them the same way.

However, Jesus treated the Romans with fairness and equality. This was shown when Jesus healed a Roman Centurion's servant.

MI TPD Cit PD

Read the story in Luke 7:1-10.

What did Jesus mean when he said, "I have never found faith like this, not even in Israel".

Why would the Jewish people have been surprised that Jesus helped this man?

Talk about the example of Jesus. Does it say anything about how we should treat other people?

Religion

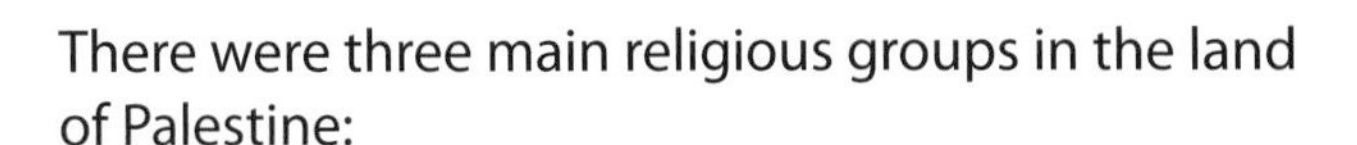

There were three main religious groups in the land of Palestine:

1) The Jews
2) The **Gentiles** (anyone who was not a Jew) – the Romans would have been regarded as Gentiles. The Romans were also regarded as pagans because they worshipped a number of different gods.
3) The **Samaritans** – Jews did not like the Samaritans.

The dislike between them went back a long way.

After the death of King Solomon, the Kingdom of Israel broke up into two parts – Israel in the north and Judah in the south.

The country was invaded by a nation called Assyria. The Assyrians treated Israel and Judah differently. They took away many of the people in Judah and sent them to **exile** in Assyria, but they settled in the north and started to live alongside the native Jews.

The people around the region of Samaria lived side by side with the Assyrians for many years and over time Jews and Assyrians intermarried.

These people of mixed race became known as **Samaritans**. Many of the Jews returned from exile in Assyria. They hated the Samaritans and thought they were **traitors** for intermarrying with the 'enemy'.

They said they were unclean and **inferior** as they were no longer pure Jews – they were of mixed race.

To add to the bad feeling, Samaritans did not keep the Jewish law.

Also Samaritans did not attend Temple worship, but built their own religious shrine at Mount Gerizim.

Mount Gerizim

For the Samaritans Mount Gerizim was a holy place. They believed it was the place God chose for the Temple to be located and not Jerusalem. They celebrated the Passover festival here. The Samaritans think that Mount Gerizim was where Isaac was nearly sacrificed by Abraham.

As a Jew, people may have expected Jesus not to like Samaritans either.

However, this was not the case at all. He helped a Samaritan (one of the ten lepers was a Samaritan, Luke 17:11-19). He even made a Samaritan the hero of one of his parables (Luke 10:25-37). The Samaritan was the one who did the right thing in comparison to the other religious leaders who had no compassion.

BC TPD Cit PD

Perform a role-play of the parable of the Good Samaritan.

Now update it. How could this happen today? What would *you* do?

JEWISH RELIGIOUS LEADERS

TPD Cit

Who are the important leaders in your life at the minute?

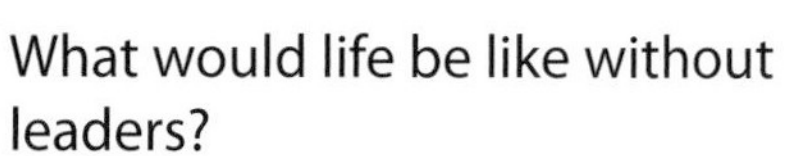

What would life be like without leaders?

We need leaders in many different areas of life. Someone has to be in charge of the school, the country, or the company.

Someone has to lead the worship in church or act as referee at a football match.

Rabbi

A **Rabbi** was (and is) not a Jewish priest, but a religious teacher and someone who could resolve disputes in matters of religious law.

At the time of Jesus the Rabbis taught in the local synagogues.

Ten or more men had to live in a town or village before a synagogue was built.

The work of the Rabbi was unpaid so many of them did other jobs too.

The Rabbi preached the sermon in the synagogue on the Sabbath and was also responsible for teaching the boys in the synagogue school.

It was the Rabbi's duty to remind the people to keep the special laws of their religion, eg ceremonial washing before prayer, and the food laws.

ICT

Use the web address below to go on a virtual tour of a Jewish synagogue.

http://www.logosre.net/ks3/worldreligions/judaismtour.htm

Pharisees

The Pharisees were a strict religious group. They were very strict about keeping every custom of the Jewish law, known as the Torah (the law of Moses).

Many of them were very proud and self-righteous, believing themselves to be more holy than the ordinary Jewish people.

The name Pharisee means 'separated one' and they often kept themselves separate from groups who they believed to be spiritually unclean, eg sinners, Gentiles, lepers.

A Pharisee

The Pharisees resented the Roman occupation of Israel because the Romans were Gentiles and did not follow the Jewish law.

The Pharisees also lived by the oral (spoken) law.

This was a series of extra rules that had been made up to explain the rules in the Torah more fully to make sure they were not broken.

For example, the Torah demanded that Jews respect the Sabbath day. In practice this involved not working or doing any unnecessary tasks from sunset on Friday until sunset on Saturday.

However the Pharisees took this a step further. For example, they would not eat an egg laid by a hen on the Sabbath day as the hen had worked to lay the egg!

The ordinary people admired the Pharisees for their devotion to God. However, Jesus criticised the Pharisees for observing these oral laws. He said they were making religion a burden to the people. (Mark 2:27)

He said that some of them were **hypocrites** because they cared more for the law than they cared for the people.

SaddMucees

The Sadducees were richer and of higher rank than the Pharisees, coming from the **aristocratic** families of the region.

Unlike the Pharisees, who resented the Romans, the Sadducees cooperated with the Romans in order to protect their wealth and lands.

The Sadducees were a small but very powerful religious group. They followed the Torah or written law closely but did not accept the oral law. They were very conservative and took the Torah literally.

They did not believe in resurrection from the dead because it was not mentioned in the Torah.

The Pharisees and Sadducees were always disagreeing with each other, but they joined forces against Jesus.

Scribes

The word scribe means 'write' or 'writer'.

At this time, when not many people could read or write, the scribes copied out the scrolls of the Old Testament. This way they became experts in the religious law.

The new laws they created to cover every part of Jewish life were passed on orally and became known as the spoken law.

The scribes also became judges, settling religious disputes. Many of the scribes were also Pharisees.

High Priest

The High Priest was the most important person amongst the religious leaders. He was the head or chief priest of the Jewish people.

The office of High Priest was **hereditary**, which means that it was handed down in his family.

ICT
MI
BC

Carry out some research to find out what kind of robes the High Priest wore.

Draw a coloured picture of him and label any of his clothes that have a special meaning.

The High Priest had an official house in the Temple. He was the only person allowed to enter the Holy of Holies in the Temple.

The Jews believe that God's presence was in this room and the High Priest entered it once a year on the Day of Atonement.

At the time of Jesus' death the High Priest was a man called **Caiaphas**.

Sanhedrin

The **Sanhedrin** was the most important religious body.

It had seventy-one members selected from amongst the Pharisees and Sadducees.

The High Priest was president of the Sanhedrin.

If a Jew committed a religious offence, he would be brought to the Sanhedrin for trial and sentencing. The Sanhedrin could not sentence anyone to death.

They also discussed and debated matters of religious importance.

MI
BC
WO

In groups, prepare a display on the religious leaders in the time of Jesus.

JESUS AND THE RELIGIOUS LEADERS

Jesus delighted the crowds with his straightforward and common-sense approach to religious teaching. He seemed to bring God near and to make serving him the most natural and exciting thing in the world.

However, this did not make him popular with everyone. The ordinary people loved him, but his popularity made the religious leaders hate him.

Many of them thought that he was leading the people astray and everywhere Jesus went they criticised the things he did and said.

Why the religious leaders were against Jesus

1. Sometimes, when he healed people he broke the rule that banned work on the Sabbath. They believed that this was breaking the Jewish law.
2. He mixed with and made friends with outcasts and spiritually unclean people like lepers and tax collectors.
3. He spoke out against the religious leaders and called them hypocrites.
4. He predicted that the Temple in Jerusalem would be destroyed.
5. He spoke with authority and claimed that his power came from God, and that God was his Father. The religious leaders didn't like this because he seemed to be claiming to have a special relationship with God.

What Jesus said about the religious leaders

MI

Read Mark 12:38-40 and write down some of the things Jesus accused the religious leaders of.

It is important to realise that Jesus did have friends amongst the religious leaders. For example Nicodemus was a religious ruler. You can read about him in John 7:50-51 and 19:38-39.

Jesus accepted that many of them were good and sincere men, but there were others who were not. Jesus' rising power and influence with the people made them jealous and determined to have Jesus **executed**.

The religious leaders accuse Jesus' disciples of working on the Sabbath

Sabbath

This is the name given by the Jews to the seventh day of the week, their holy day, which begins at sunset on Friday and continues to sunset on Saturday.

For Jews it is very important to observe the Sabbath. It is marked by rest from work and ordinary weekly activities. There are also synagogue services and special rituals in the home.

Read Matthew 12:1-14.

Both of these stories show that the religious leaders believed that obeying the law was more important than helping people.

Jesus had a very different opinion. He said that mercy and helpfulness were more important than obeying strict laws.

Com
MI
BC
WO

As well as the passage already read, look at these ones: Mark 7:1-15, Mark 12:13-17, Mark 12:18-27.

In groups write and present a piece of drama outlining the accusations the religious leaders made against Jesus and the things he said in his defence.

Imagine that you are in a courtroom. You should have a judge, prosecutor, defence lawyer, Jesus, some religious leaders, eyewitnesses, etc.

JEWISH RELIGIOUS CUSTOMS

Within Judaism there are a number of traditional customs that must be followed in order to show respect for God and the Law.

During morning prayer every Jewish man is supposed to wear a shawl called a **tallit**. It has a tassel at each corner that represents the four consonants of God's name in Hebrew – **YAHWEH.** Each tassel has many strands which stand for the 613 regulations of the Torah or written law.

A tallit

A Jewish boy receives his tallit at his **Bar Mitzvah** ceremony when he is aged 13. A girl has a **Bat Mitzvah** ceremony when she is 12.

The word 'Bar' means 'son' and 'Bat' means daughter. 'Mitzvah' means 'commandment', therefore they become a son or daughter of the Commandments or Law.

A boy is now believed to be old enough to understand the teachings of his religion. As well as the tallit a boy will also receive his **Siddur** or prayer book.

The boy's Bar Mitzvah will take place on the Sabbath in the Synagogue, and he will have to read a portion of the Torah in Hebrew to the congregation.

The reading will be taken from one of the Scrolls that are kept in a special place at the front of the synagogue called the **Ark**.

Tefillin

After a boy has had his Bar Mitzvah, he has to wear **tefillin** or **phylacteries** when he says his daily prayers. These are small leather boxes with four passages from the Torah inside them. They must be worn on the forehead as a reminder to keep God in his mind at all times.

The tefillin are also worn on the inside of the arm, which is near to the heart, and is a reminder to keep God's law in his heart.

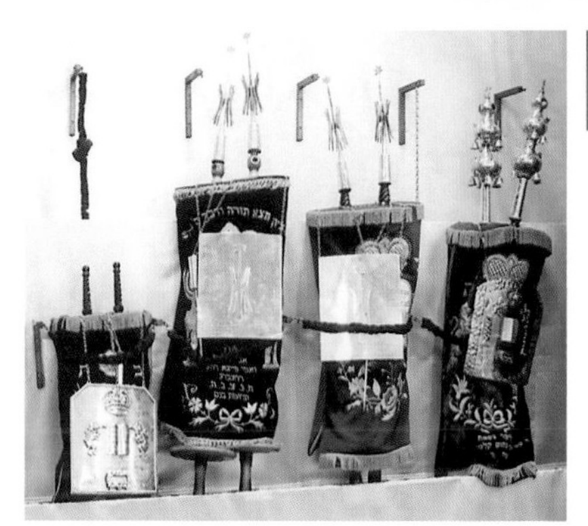
Torah scrolls in the Belfast Synagogue

The Torah can be found in every synagogue and it is written on scrolls. These are treated with great respect as they are viewed as the word of God. When they are not in use, they are carefully placed inside very decorative covers and are stored in the Ark.

When reading the scrolls a special pointer called a **Yad** is used to avoid touching the scrolls.

Jewish men also wear a skullcap, the **kippah**, as a sign of their respect to God. It is compulsory for men to cover their heads in the synagogue.

At the entrance of most Jewish homes there is a little wooden or metal box on the doorpost called the **mezuzah**. Inside it there is a small scroll containing the words of the **shema**, which is a Jewish statement of faith. This is a reminder of God's presence in the home. The father will touch the mezuzah as he leaves the house and when he returns to it, saying a short prayer: "May God keep my going out and my coming in".

A mezuzah

One of the oldest symbols of the Jewish faith is the **menorah**, a seven-branched candlestick used in the Temple. The priest lit the menorah in the sanctuary every evening and cleaned it out every morning, replacing the wicks and putting fresh olive oil into the cups.

The menorah is a symbol of the nation of Israel, the Jews, being "a light to the nations". The special menorah used at **Hanukkah** is called a **hanukiah**. It has nine branches.

You can read more about Judaism in *Local People, Global Faiths*, Book 1, (Colourpoint).

MI

1 Write down three things about the tallit.

2 Make up a sentence that includes the words Bar Mitzvah and Siddur.

3 Explain why the tefillin are worn on the inner arm and forehead.

4 The Jews have great respect for God's word. Write down two things that they do to show this.

5 What is the Mezuzah?

6 What is the Menorah?

Culture

HOMES

Think about the different types of homes we have in our country today. How many can you think of?

At the time of Jesus, ordinary people had very little choice about the sort of house they lived in. They were nearly all the same.

A house in Palestine was built out of mud bricks or stone covered in mortar or lime mud. Before the building could begin the bricks had to be made. A shallow hole was dug and filled with water and clay, to which straw was added. All of this was mixed together by the people walking on them. Then the mixture was pressed into wooden moulds and allowed to bake in the sun.

Most Jewish families lived in one-roomed houses with a flat roof. Heavy wooden beams were laid across the walls and covered with branches, reeds, mud and grass to create a strong roof. It was important that this was constructed carefully as the family used the roof every day. Sometimes they even slept on it in warm weather.

Inside the house the dirt or clay floor was divided into two areas. The family lived, worked and slept on a raised platform at one end of the room, and their animals lived in the other section.

A hole was dug in the floor for the fire and the smoke made its way out of the door and the small windows. It was so dark inside the house that a lamp had to be kept lit all the time.

Many families did not have much furniture. For example, they did not have beds, but slept on straw mats that were rolled up during the day.

BC

Draw your own picture of the inside of an ordinary house in Palestine. Would you like to live in a house like this? Would you miss some things?

If so, what would you miss?

FAMILY LIFE

Male and female roles

MI
TPD
PD

Make a list of all the jobs there are in keeping a house and family. Think of things like ironing, cleaning windows, cutting the grass. It will be a long list!

Write it all out and now write beside each one who does it, or who you think should do it.

Discuss your results.

MI
TPD
WO

Do a survey in your class. Ask how many people live in each pupil's house. Present your findings as a bar graph.

The family includes more than just the parents and children. There are also grandparents, aunts, uncles and cousins.

This is known as the extended family and in Jesus' time it was not unusual to find all of these people sharing the same house – a one-roomed house!

The eldest male was the head of the family and was responsible for making the important decisions.

Women had a very busy life. They had to bake bread, fetch water from the local well, make all the clothes for the family, look after the children and find time to sell goods in the marketplace as well.

Women were always expected to obey their husbands.

Children had to do chores around the home, for example, collecting wood for the fire or caring for the animals.

Every child's education began at home, but when they were six, boys were sent to the synagogue school where they were taught by the rabbi. They would learn about the history and geography of their country, as well as the Jewish scriptures, or Torah.

Jewish girls, no matter how clever they were, did not go to school. Instead they stayed at home with their mothers and learned how to look after the home and children.

From the time they were born, girls were under the authority of their father until they married, when they came under the authority of their husband.

A man could have more than one wife if he wished and he could divorce his wife quite easily. However, it was very difficult for a woman to get a divorce.

Usually only men were allowed to own property in Palestine. The one exception was when a father died without having sons. The property then passed to the oldest girl.

Adultery was regarded as a serious offence. Sometimes a woman suspected of this was given the jealousy test. She was brought to the priest and clay and water were mixed in a bowl.

The woman drank the mixture and everyone waited to see what happened. If the woman's stomach became swollen she was said to be guilty and could face execution by stoning.

You can read this in Number 5:11-31.

Birth of a baby

As soon as a baby was born it was rubbed all over with salt and wrapped from head to toe in swaddling bands. This prevented the baby from moving its arms and legs as they believed this could damage its developing bones.

Men were not allowed to be present at the birth of a baby and mothers gave birth at home. There weren't any hospitals.

If the baby was a boy the celebrations were always greater as boys were thought to be of more importance than girls.

A couple's first child was believed to belong to God so when it was four weeks old the child was 'bought back' from God by paying five silver **shekels** to the Temple.

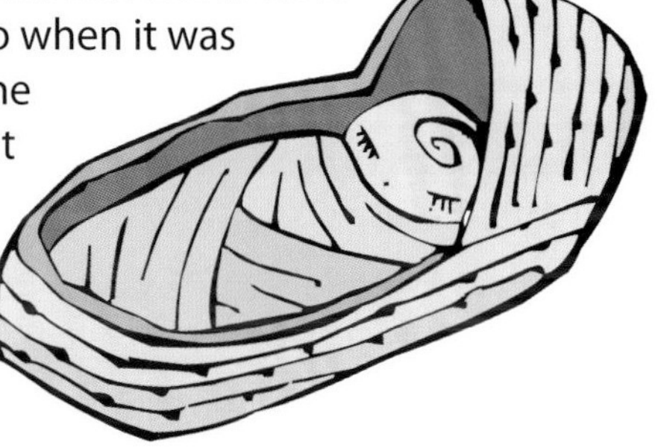

MI

What is a shekel?

Marriage

Parents usually arranged the marriage of their children.

A sum of money called the 'bride price' was agreed and given to the bride's family by the groom's parents. In turn her parents gave the girl a **dowry**.

The two people were now **betrothed** and it was very difficult to break this, even if the couple wanted to. Being betrothed was even more binding than being engaged today.

A betrothal could last months or years.

MI TPD

Think of some of the traditions associated with weddings today. A white dress; flowers; something new, old, borrowed, blue; rings.

Talk about them and try to work out why we have them.

On the wedding day the bride's hair was plaited and silk was woven through it. Coins were then attached to the silk. There could be more than a thousand coins in her hair. This was part of her dowry to her new husband.

A Jewish wedding ceremony today

The wedding celebration was very colourful, with garlands of flowers and lots of lamps. It could last for up to seven days.

As the bridegroom left his house to collect the bride, women came out and lit lamps along the procession route.

It was a great insult if a lamp went out. It was almost a bad omen upon the marriage.

MI TPD Cit

In pairs, discuss the Jewish wedding and a wedding in our country today.

What things are the same?

What things are different?

Funerals

As soon as someone died, a time of mourning began. Relatives tore their clothes and wore sackcloth and ashes as an outward sign of their sorrow. (Daniel 9:3)

Burial usually took place within eight hours as the heat made it difficult to keep the body for longer than that.

Poor people were often buried together. Wealthier people may have had a family tomb.

MI BC

Imagine that you are a Jewish boy or girl living at the time of Jesus.

Write a diary entry about what is going on in your life. What has happened in your day? Try to put in lots of things.

Use the things that you have learned about homes, family life and so on, to help you.

FOOD

Two common problems for farmers were drought and locusts, either of which could destroy their crops. But if the conditions were good there were lots of different things to eat.

There were lots of fruit and vegetables. **Pulses** like lentils formed an important part of the diet. Women ground corn and used it to bake bread.

To sweeten food, raisins, dates and honey were added. Meat was a luxury and was eaten only on special occasions. People who lived near the Sea of Galilee would also have eaten fish.

Food Laws

'**Kashrut**' is the name for the food laws in the Jewish religion.

'Kosher' means that a food is permitted or 'clean', while anything 'unclean' (such as pork and shellfish) is strictly forbidden.

These food laws applied when Jesus was alive and are still very important to many Jews today.

The law also contains a ban on eating the blood of an animal, therefore the animal has to be killed in a special way and the blood drained from it before it can be eaten.

Fish with scales are clean while other fish and shellfish are not. This gives protection from food poisoning which can be caused by creatures which feed on silt on the sea bed.

Jews will not mix meat and milk, either for dishes that combine the two ingredients or following a meat dish with a milk pudding. The scriptural reason for this is probably the prohibition on "boiling a kid in its mother's milk". (Exodus 23:19)

Utensils (pots, pans, plates, etc) must also be kosher. If you cook chicken soup in a saucepan, the pan becomes meat and you cannot use it to heat milk. It is also necessary to use different basins for washing milk and meat utensils.

MI

Pigs are unclean so Jews should not eat pork. Read Leviticus 11:1-23. Which foods are kosher?

TPD PD

Jewish people have lots of food laws.

How easy would it be to keep them where you live?

Do you know of any food laws in other world faiths?

TPD Cit

Imagine that a Jewish boy or girl has moved to your area.

Write down two problems or challenges that they might have to deal with if they are trying to keep the kosher food regulations.

MI TPD Cit

Look at the menu below. Are there any foods which a Jewish boy or girl should not eat?

Snacks

A ham sandwich (no butter)

Chicken burger

Cheese burger

Roast Beef with lettuce and tomato salad

Lunch Menu

Cod and chips

Hamburger and chips

Lasagne and chips

Today's Specials

Roast turkey dinner followed by custard and apple tart.

Roast beef dinner followed by steamed fruit

Chicken stir-fry

Roast lamb served on a bed of cheesy vegetables

RELIGIOUS FESTIVALS

MI
BC
TPD

Name some of the important festivals that are celebrated by Christians.

Find out why Christians celebrate these. What important events to they remember?

Make a wall display explaining what each one is about.

The Jews celebrated three main festivals. All of them were linked to important events in their history.

These festivals were called 'foot' festivals because as many people as possible travelled to Jerusalem to celebrate them.

They are still celebrated today.

Passover (Pesach)

This is one of the most important festivals.

It is held in the spring and celebrates the time when the Jews were in the land of Egypt and Moses wanted to lead them back to their own country.

You learned about this on page 30.

Pentecost

Fifty days after the Passover, the Jews celebrate **Pentecost**, which is a harvest celebration.

During this festival the Jews are reminded that it is God who provided for their every need.

Tabernacles (Booths)

This festival also emphasises the importance of giving thanks to God.

At the time of Jesus, people celebrated by putting tents up and living in them for eight days. They decorated these temporary homes with fruit, vegetables and flowers.

Many Jews today still do this in their homes.

The festival is to remember how God looked after the Jews when they were wandering for forty years in the wilderness on their way to the promised land. (You learnt about this on pages 32-39.)

That's 'Hanukkah' in Hebrew!

Hanukkah

Hanukkah, (or Chanukah) which means 'dedication', is also called 'The Festival of Lights' and lasts eight days.

The festival falls somewhere between the end of November and the end of December.

Hanukkah begins on the 25th day of the Hebrew month of Kislev, but the starting date on the western calendar varies from year to year.

The festival remembers a victory by the Jews over the Greeks in Old Testament times.

iStockphoto/charles shapiro

A Hanukkah candlestick.

The history of Hanukkah

The Greeks ruled the land of Palestine in the second century BC and they treated the Jews very badly.

The Jews didn't like the Greeks, especially when they took control of the Temple and made it into a place to worship the Greek gods.

Many of the Jews were determined to get their Temple back and a man named Judah formed an army to fight the Greeks. His army was called the 'Maccabees' which means hammers.

What does this name suggest about the type of men in Judah's army?

The fighting between the Greeks and the Maccabees lasted for three years until eventually Judah and his men won. They reclaimed the Temple for the Jews, removed all the symbols of the Greek gods and put back the Jewish ones.

One of the things that Judah returned to the Temple was a special lamp called a **Ner Tamid**. In every Jewish place of worship this lamp is constantly burned to remind worshippers of the presence of God.

When Judah and his men came to light the lamp they realised that they had only enough oil to last one day, but miraculously the lamp stayed alight for eight days.

To remind Jews of this miracle and the belief that God is with them at all times, Jews light candles during the Hanukkah festival.

This is the most important ritual. The candles are on a special nine-branched candle holder called a hanukiah. Each night, one more candle is added.

iStockphoto/howard sandler

The middle candle, called the 'shamash', is used to light each of the other candles and it is lit every night.

Therefore, on the first night of Hanukkah, two candles are lit (the shamash and the candle for the first night) and on the last night, there are nine lit candles.

Another tradition is to play the **dreidel** game. A dreidel is a four-sided top. The dreidel is used for a gambling game in which each letter represents a different amount of money (or whatever...) won or lost.

Another common Hanukkah practice is giving gifts or gelt (money) to children.

Com
ICT
MI
BC
WO
Cit

Imagine that you were living in Palestine at the time of Jesus.

Design a travel brochure advertising your country.

You should highlight the things that would be appealing to tourists.

You could find pictures from magazines and travel brochures. Think about the kind of language you would use in a brochure and what pictures you would use.

Is there anything you would *not* put in a travel brochure?

OR

Make a 'Wish you were here' style presentation about Israel. Ask your teacher to make a video of it. You will need to think carefully about your costumes, scenes, etc.

Jesus and his relationship with people

Disciples

FRIENDS

TPD
PD

What is a friend?

Write down what you think a friend is.

A friend is …

Read out your definitions. Are they very different? Are a lot of them almost the same?

TPD
PD

Is it easier to *have* a friend or to *be* a friend?

What is the difference?

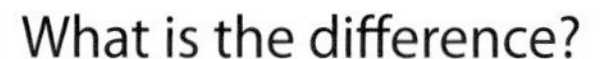

A friend is someone who knows everything there is to know about me and still likes me!

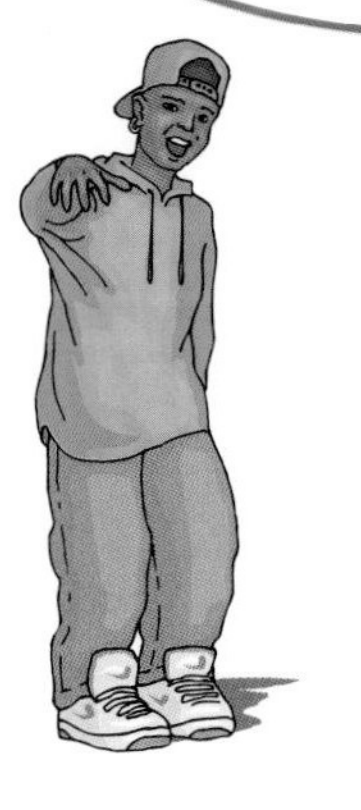

TPD
SM
WO
PD

Are there times when loyalty can be tested?

Friends are loyal to each other but what is the right thing to do in these situations? Justify the choices you make.

What would you do if …?

Situation 1

Your close friend asks you to tell her/his mother that they are staying at your house for a sleep over when they are really going to an all-night party with people his/her parents don't approve of.

Situation 2

You discover that a good friend has started smoking.

Situation 3

It is Thursday afternoon and you have finished PE. You see two of your friends messing around in the changing rooms. They accidentally break the door. The next day at school everyone is questioned about the damage to find out who did it.

SM
PD

1 Is it important to choose your friends carefully?
2 Read the following quote and try to explain what it means.

One rotten fish and one fresh fish equals two rotten fish.

3 Think of some of the soaps on TV. List situations in which friends have been a bad influence or a good influence.

Jesus and his friends – the disciples

Jesus needed company as he travelled around preaching and teaching. He also needed people to help him with his work and to carry on his work after he died.

The word **disciple** means 'learner' or 'follower'.

Jesus chose 12 men to be his friends throughout the three years of his ministry.

MI
WO

Can you name any of the disciples?

With a partner see how many you can name. Then see if your class has named them all.

MI

Try to find out why Jesus chose twelve disciples.

This number is very significant in Judaism.

Jesus calls the disciples

At home you might be asked to help out. At school you might be asked to join a team and play your part. Your friends might want you to listen to them and help them out if they need it.

Jesus calls the fishermen

MI

Read the story in Matthew 4:18-22 and answer these questions.

1 Name the first two disciples that Jesus called.

2 How were these two men related?

3 What was their occupation?

4 On the shore of which sea did Jesus call them?

5 The next two disciples who followed him were James and John. What was their father called?

6 Jesus told them that he would make them 'Fishers of _______' (Fill in the missing word).

7 Explain what you think Jesus' words in verse 19 mean.

The fishermen were obviously impressed by Jesus because they immediately left their fishing boats and businesses and followed him.

Responding to a call

Sir Ernest Shackleton was born in County Kildare in the 19th century. He was the explorer who went to the South Pole and who died and is buried on South Georgia. Find out where this is.

Before the expedition it is said that Shackleton put an advertisement into a newspaper which read:

'Men wanted for hazardous journey. Small wages, bitter cold. Long months of complete darkness. Constant danger, safe return doubtful. Honour and recognition in case of success.'

Would you have responded to this advertisement? If so, what would have appealed to you? If you would not have responded, why not?

Five thousand people replied and Ernest Shackleton selected twenty-seven to join him on his expedition.

TPD

Why do you think these men left everything to follow Jesus?

What reasons could there be?

Com
MI
BC
TPD

Divide the class into two halves. Imagine that you are Peter.

One half must answer for Peter. The other half must ask him questions.

What would you like to ask him?

Many people may have been surprised that Jesus chose such ordinary people to be his followers. These men would not have been educated like the religious leaders, but they had many other qualities that were more important.

TPD

What sort of men do you think Jesus looked for to be his disciples?

Do you think these men had to give up anything to follow Jesus?

What problems would they face as followers of Jesus?

Jesus calls Levi/Matthew the tax collector

This role-play is taken from Mark 2 :13–17. Pick people to play each role.

Narrator 1: Jesus went back to the shore of Lake Galilee and a crowd of people followed him. As he was walking along he spotted a tax collector called Levi sitting in his office. Levi was also called Matthew by some people. Jesus spoke to him.

Jesus: Follow me.

Narrator 2: Levi immediately got up and followed Jesus. He said to Jesus:

Levi: Lord, you must come to my house for a meal.

Narrator 3: Later that day Jesus went to Levi's house for a meal and many tax collectors and other outcasts came and joined them. Having a meal with someone showed you were happy to be their friend. Many people were surprised that Jesus, a Jew, would mix with a sinner like Levi.

Narrator 4: Tax collectors were unpopular with the Jewish people because they worked for the Romans. They also overcharged the people, keeping some of the money for themselves. So they were looked on as thieves and sinners and were viewed as spiritually unclean. For these reasons the ordinary people did not mix with tax collectors, for fear of risking their own spiritual purity. Some religious leaders saw Jesus at Levi's house and asked his disciples:

Religious leaders: Why does he eat with such people? Does he not realise that he is mixing with sinners and outcasts?

Jesus: I hear what you ask! It is not the healthy that need a doctor but the sick. I have not come to call respectable people, but outcasts.

Narrator 5: Jesus meant that he had come to save all kinds of people, especially the sinners who were most in need.

MI
BC

Imagine that you are Levi.

Write an account of all that happened on the day Jesus asked you to be a disciple. Include your feelings and what you thought.

BC

Pretend you are one of the disciples of Jesus.

Write a postcard home to your family, telling them how Jesus called you, how your life has changed, what you are doing, and so on.

ICT
MI
BC
SM
EfE

Design a job application pack for a disciple of Jesus.

Include the qualifications, characteristics and so on, that you think a disciple would have to have.

You should also include a brief description of what the job will involve. Mention things like the salary, accommodation, duties and any **perks**, eg opportunity to travel. What else could you include?

Present your job application pack to your teacher in a folder or large envelope. Wordprocess it if you can and set it out well.

MI
WO

Quiz

Divide your class into teams. Hand out as many Bibles as you can. When your teacher calls out one of these questions, the team which calls out the answer first gets a point.

1 Which disciple collected taxes? (Matthew 10:3)

2 Which was Andrew's brother? (Matthew 10:2)

3 Which two were called the Sons of Thunder? (Mark 3:17)

4 Which disciple betrayed Jesus? (Matthew 26:14-16)

5 Which one doubted the resurrection? (John 20:24-29)

6 Which one is often referred to as the 'disciple whom Jesus loved'? (John 20:2)

7 Which three disciples were with Jesus at the transfiguration? (Mark 9:2-3)

8 Which disciple said that eight months' wages would not be enough to buy bread to feed the great crowd? (John 6:5-7)

Women

MI
TPD
EfE
PD

Look at the following occupations.

Say whether you think it would be more suitable for a man or a woman.

Justify your answer. First say who you think of as usually doing the job. Then say if you think it *could* be done by both men and women.

Doctor	Tailor
Plumber	Member of clergy
Refuse collector	Mechanic
Fire fighter	Bus driver
Hairdresser	Secretary
Bricklayer	Painter

JESUS' ATTITUDE TO WOMEN

Jesus' attitude towards women was very unusual for a Jew and teacher (Rabbi) of his day.

As you have already learned, women were not as important as men in Jewish society.

But Jesus respected women and allowed them to become his followers, serve him and listen to his teaching. He was not afraid of criticism from others for his actions.

Jesus broke through the **prejudice** displayed towards women and he often spoke to them and helped them.

Jesus at the house of Mary and Martha

This role-play is taken from Luke 10:38-42. Act it out in class.

Narrator: Jesus had some friends who lived in Bethany, a village near Jerusalem. They were Mary, Martha and their brother Lazarus. Jesus often called to stay and they looked forward to his visits even though the day before he came was hectic with cleaning, washing and cooking. The following scene took place on a day when Jesus came to visit.

Martha: (In a very cross voice) For goodness sake Mary, you are such a silly girl. You know that Jesus is coming to visit today and you are doing nothing to help me. What is your problem?

Mary: I'm sorry Martha, I start a job but then I get so excited about the idea of Jesus coming to visit that I forget what I'm doing. I'm looking forward to hearing the stories about the people he's healed and the exciting things he and the disciples have done.

Martha: Well, that's just not good enough, Mary. Do you think Jesus will be impressed if he sits down to eat and there's no water in the jug and no bread baked? I think not! Stop daydreaming and do something useful. Go and sweep the doorstep.

Mary: But I think I hear voices, Martha. I'll just go and check … I won't be long. (Mary runs out the door)

Martha: (Mutters to herself) Of all the lazy, irresponsible girls. Well, I will just *tell* Jesus that she has given me no help at all.

Narrator: As Martha continues to huff and puff, Mary excitedly bursts back through the door.

Mary: Martha, quick! Jesus has arrived. Come on, hurry up! He and his friends are coming down the road.

Martha: Oh no! The bread isn't ready and the meat isn't cooked. Mary, I need water from the well – go and get some.

Mary: I can't go now, Jesus is here. Come on. Leave the dinner.

Narrator: Mary ran out to meet Jesus and fetched him a bowl of water to rinse his feet. Then she sat down and listened to Jesus talking to Lazarus and the others. She loved to hear him talk about his Father and the Kingdom of Heaven. Mary forgot all about Martha and the help she needed in the house. When Martha appeared she saw Mary sitting doing nothing and she was furious. She was so hot, and tired, and angry that she burst out.

Martha: It's not fair! Mary does nothing to help me. I do all the work and she just sits there pretending she's so good. Master, tell her to get up and give me a hand.

Jesus: Oh Martha, you worry about so many little things that do not matter. It is Mary who is doing what is right. She wants to learn about God's love. You must come and sit down too. The dinner can wait.

Narrator: Martha came and sat down, but she was still angry and hurt that Jesus had taken Mary's side. But soon she became interested in what Jesus was saying and she forgot about the bread and the water and the row.

Martha: You know Jesus, you are right. Work isn't everything. Other things, like making time for God, are more important.

TPD
SM
EfE
PD

Did Jesus mean that working hard is wrong? What do you think he meant?

What did he believe was more important than Martha's fussing?

Who's side would you be on in this story?

Why would some people want to work all the time?

What important things can people shut out of their lives by working all the time?

Jesus at the home of Simon the Pharisee

Read the story – Luke 7:37-50

TPD
Cit
PD

When a visitor comes to your house, what things do you and your family do to show them that they are welcome?

Can you find out some of the different ways people greet each other in other countries?

A Pharisee named Simon invited Jesus to dine at his home.

A well-mannered host would always greet a respected guest with a kiss of peace.

One of the servants would be called to bathe the guest's feet with water to wash away the dust from the roads.

A drop of perfumed oil was put on the guest's head to refresh him after the hot and tiring journey.

Simon didn't do any of this when Jesus arrived. Why do you think he didn't?

As they were eating, a bad woman came in. She began to cry and the tears dropped on Jesus' feet. She then used her long hair to dry his feet and poured precious ointment on them.

Com TPD

The two debtors

Two men owed money to a money lender. One owed 500 silver coins and the other 50 silver coins. Realising that neither of them could pay the money back, the lender forgave them both and cancelled their debt.

Jesus asked Simon:

Which one of them will love him more?

Simon replied:

The one who was forgiven more.

Jesus agreed.

Talk about this story.

What was the point Jesus was making?

Compare Simon with the woman who cried. Were their attitudes to Jesus different?

TPD

Why were the religious leaders at Simon's house surprised when Jesus allowed this woman to touch him?

MI TPD BC Cit PD

Women in Jewish society did not have equality with men.

Has this situation changed for women in the twenty-first century?

Find out about any countries or circumstances today where women are not treated the same as men. Present your findings to the class.

Simon thought that if Jesus really was a prophet he would realise what type of woman this was and wouldn't let her near him.

Perhaps Jesus saw the criticism on Simon's face. Instead of scolding him, Jesus told the story of two debtors.

Outcasts

BEING AN OUTCAST

TPD

What do you notice about these two photos?

iStockphoto/mandygodbehear

iStockphoto/Karen Grotzinner

TPD EfE Cit PD

Do you think of any of these people as 'different'?

What feelings and abilities do these people share with you?

What feelings and abilities do they not share with you?

The Odyssey Arena

Com MI TPD SM WO PD

The great balloon debate

Imagine that your group has received a special invitation to a pop concert at the Odyssey Arena in Belfast.

Only one person can go! Who will it be? You must decide!

Each person in your group must take on the role of one of the people pictured above. You are allowed to make three statements about why you should be allowed to attend this special event.

The group must then decide fairly who has to leave the balloon until one person is left to travel to the Odyssey Arena!

TPD SM Cit PD

How could you, or a group you belong to, make someone feel like an outcast?

Has this ever happened to you? If you want to talk about it say:

What happened?

What did you do?

How did you feel?

How do you feel about it now?

What could have prevented it?

TPD BC WO Cit

Think about all the reasons people are outcast today. Brainstorm them with your partner.

Now role-play a real or invented situation based on being an outcast.

MI PD

Research

Investigate the work of the **NSPCC** and their campaign to 'beat the bully'.

Com MI BC TPD WO Cit

Divide into groups.

Your task is to create a collage to represent outcasts today. You can use pictures and words. Your teacher will tell how long you have to do this.

When you have finished your collage, present it to the rest of the class explaining your choice of pictures and words.

Each group should decide on two things they like about each finished collage.

Discuss one thing that could improve each collage.

OUTCASTS AT THE TIME OF JESUS

At the time of Jesus many people were left out or **excluded** because of race, religion, gender or disability.

MI

Who were these outcasts? Find out who they were by looking up these references.

Luke 5:27-32 Luke 5:12-14

Luke 10:30-37 Luke 18:35-43

The greedy man

Jesus made friends with people who were outcasts. They were not popular.

Read Luke 12:13-21, the story of Jesus meeting with a greedy man.

This greedy man lived in Jericho and Jesus was passing through here on his way to Jerusalem which was about 32 kilometres away.

Why did Zacchaeus' job make him unpopular?

1. Tax collectors were hated by most of Jewish society. They were seen as traitors because they worked for the Romans.
2. As well as collecting the taxes for the Roman Empire, the tax collectors also stole from ordinary people. They did this by adding an extra charge to the tax being collected.
3. Tax collectors were seen as sinners and therefore spiritually impure.

TPD

Why did Jesus accept Zacchaeus as one of his followers?

Com TPD WO

Zacchaeus in the hot seat

Carry out this activity in pairs.

One person takes on the character of Zacchaeus and takes the 'hot seat' to answer questions.

The other person has to ask 'Zacchaeus' challenging questions.

What would you ask him?

MI

1 What was Zacchaeus' job?
2 In what town did Jesus meet Zacchaeus?
3 Write down a word to describe Zacchaeus' financial state.
4 Why could Zacchaeus not see Jesus?
5 What did Zacchaeus do to ensure that he did see Jesus?
6 What did Jesus say to Zacchaeus?
7 Many of the religious leaders complained when they saw Jesus going with Zacchaeus to his house. Why would they have been annoyed?
8 Zacchaeus was a changed man after his meeting with Jesus. What did he do to show that he was a reformed character?

Com BC

Write a letter to your cousin explaining what happened the day Jesus came to Jericho.

Explain who Zacchaeus is and how he was changed.

The Ten Lepers

MI TPD SM Cit

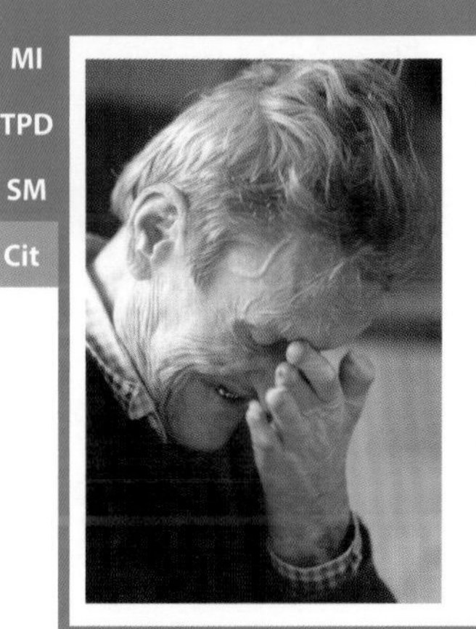

What do you see in this picture?

What could you do to help this man?

How would you feel if you had to sit next to this man?

The person in this picture has a disease which was much feared in Bible times. It is called **leprosy**.

The treatment of lepers in Bible times

1. **Lepers** were not allowed to trade in the marketplace.
2. They were not allowed to attend synagogue or Temple worship.
3. Lepers could not work because of the effects of leprosy on their hands and feet.
4. Lepers had to ring a bell and shout "unclean" as they walked along.
5. They were not allowed to wash, had to wear ragged clothes and were not allowed to comb their hair.
6. Lepers had to leave their homes and families to live in colonies on the edge of towns and villages.

How did Jesus treat lepers?

TPD

Do you think Jesus treated lepers in the same way as everyone else treated them?

Read the story of Jesus healing ten lepers in Luke 17:11-19.

As Jesus was travelling towards Jerusalem he passed through Samaria and Galilee. As he was entering a village he met a leper colony.

TPD

Why did the men stand at a distance?

What was significant about the man who returned to Jesus?

Leprosy today

Leprosy is still around in the 21st century and is still a big problem in developing countries.

In 2006 over 300,000 new leprosy cases were identified. Around 70% of new cases were in India.

ICT

MI

The work of the Leprosy Mission

Go to an internet search engine and type in 'www.tlm-ni.org'

You will need to navigate the site to find the information!

1 What is the address and telephone number of the Leprosy Mission in Northern Ireland?

2 Record your visitor number to the web site.

3 What Bible verse is used by the Leprosy Mission on their web site?

4 In how many countries is leprosy found today?

5 Name two countries with the most cases of leprosy.

6 What are the signs of leprosy?

7 What was the most interesting thing you learnt on the Leprosy Mission web site?

8 What else did you learn?

Wellesley Bailey – Leprosy Mission

How did it begin?

Wellesley Bailey was born in Ireland and lived in Dublin. When he was young, he heard that there was a fortune to be made from digging gold in Australia. In 1866, aged 20, he decided to go there. On the Sunday evening before his journey he went to Church. The service made him think. In his cabin later that night he knelt down and gave his life to Jesus.

Wellesley did not make his fortune in Australia or New Zealand so he returned home. His father was disappointed with his son and moaned "Why didn't you join the army like your brothers?"

Some time later, Wellesley's brother Christopher invited Wellesley to join him in the army, in India. Wellesley stayed with a German missionary called Reverend Reuther while in India and began to feel called into missionary work also.

In 1869, at the age of 23, Wellesley joined the American Presbyterian Mission in Punjab, where he worked with a Dr Morrison and became involved in teaching. One day he was invited to join Dr Morrison in visiting some leprosy sufferers, the unclean of society.

The sight of these people shocked him. He said, "I almost shuddered, yet at the same time I was fascinated. I feel if ever there is a special Christian work in this world, it must be among these sufferers. I must bring them the Good News about Jesus who loved and cared for leprosy sufferers while he was on earth."

Wellesley worked for some time with leprosy sufferers and wrote about his work to his fiancée Alice, in Dublin. Alice later joined him in India where they married and worked in the Punjab region until Alice's poor health meant they had to return to England.

Visiting his sisters in Dublin, Wellesley told them of his work among leprosy sufferers in India.

The sisters promised to raise £30 a year to help leprosy sufferers. Within two years they had raised £1000! Friends and supporters in Dublin formed a Society known as 'The Mission to Lepers in India'. Wellesley and Alice were sent by the Church of Scotland to work at the foot of the Himalayas in India. They built shelters for those with leprosy.

They used the money raised by Wellesley's sisters to help other missionaries set up shelters for leprosy patients and their families.

Wellesley died aged 91 in 1937. The Society is now a charity called 'The Leprosy Mission'. It works in 29 countries bringing help and healing to over 300,000 people.

A leprosy sufferer

MI

Here are some people who were called by God and mentioned in the Bible:

Exodus 3:1-6 and 10-12 (Moses)

1 Samuel 3:1-10 and 19-21 (Samuel)

Isaiah 6:1-9 (Isaiah)

Acts 9:1-18 (Paul)

Read about each and write down how they were called and what their reaction was.

Com TPD WO Cit

In groups, discuss and note down your answers to these questions.

1 Do you think God still calls people into mission work today?
2 What kind of people does he call?
3 How are they trained?
4 What type of training do they need?
5 Where would they get the training?
6 Do you know of a church which is involved in mission work?

The Good Samaritan

The story of the Good Samaritan is a **parable**. You might like to read about the Samaritans again, on pages 50-51.

MI

Find out what these words mean:

Racism

Parable

Levite

Priest (at the time of Jesus)

MI TPD PD

Read Luke 10:25-37.

1 Why would a Jew have been so shocked by this story?
2 What lessons is Jesus trying to teach to the people around him?
3 What lessons might Christians today learn from this parable?
4 What do *you* think about what the Good Samaritan did?
5 Why did Jesus make a Samaritan the hero of the story?
6 Who do you think he might make the hero if he were to tell the story to us today?

BC

Write your own modern day version of the Good Samaritan.

Remember to include a hero, a victim and two people who walked on by!

BC

It's possible that a shepherd saw the man being beaten up.

What would he have seen? How might he have felt?.

TPD

Can you think of any television programmes or films where people have faced discrimination because of their religion or race?

BC
WO

Freeze frame activity

Your teacher will put you into pairs and will re-read verses 33 and 34 of Luke 10.

Discuss how these verses should be acted out.

Act out the scene and when your teacher says "Freeze!", you have to freeze just as you are. When she says "Continue!" you must start up again.

MI
BC
TPD
Cit

Research

Find out about rock star Bono from U2.

What has he done to stop poverty?

How has he influenced public opinion?

What are U2's most famous songs? What are they about?

Why did Bono become involved in the Jubilee 2000 campaign?

How has he helped change people's opinions?

Make a wall display about him.

ICT
MI
Cit

Charities – the facts

In this activity you are going to find out some basic facts about charities in the UK.

Using the web site www.guidestar.org find out some basic facts about charities in the UK. The charity knowledge section of the web site will help you complete this task.

1 What is a charity?
2 What things do charities do?
3 What types of people work for charities?
4 What is the income of UK charities? What do they spend the money on?
5 Where does the money come from?

Christians believe that everybody is equally important, no matter who they are, or where they are from.

BC
Cit

Make a poster to show what Christians believe their attitude should be towards outcasts in society.

ICT
MI
BC
WO
Cit

Charity Presentation

In groups find out about a charity.

For example:

Tearfund, Cafod, Christian Aid, Samaritan's Purse, Trocaire, or another one you know of.

Find the web site of the charity you choose. Draw their logo.

PowerPoint presentation on your chosen charity. A simple way to do this is to think of the five 'Ws'. You could find out:

When the charity began

Where the charity works

What the charity does and ***why*** they do it

Who works for the charity

ICT
MA
MI
Cit

Charity fundraising

Visit the web site: www.charityfacts.org then click 'Fundraising', then 'The cost of fundraising'.

1 How much does it cost a charity to raise a pound?
2 How much money is spent on working with existing supporters?
3 How much does it cost to recruit new supporters?
4 How much money do they make out of their supporters long term?

MI
TPD
Cit

Can you list 10 charities that work in Northern Ireland today?

When you have made your list, have a look at it.

How many of these charities have a link with Christianity? Tick them!

TPD
SM
PD

Walking debate

"Christians should always fight against prejudice."

Imagine a line down the length of your classroom. One end means you strongly agree with the statement above. The other end means you strongly disagree with it.

Find a place in the line which corresponds to your opinion.

Be ready to explain your position if you are asked.

Case study: TREVOR HUDDLESTON

Trevor Huddleston was an Anglican Archbishop who spent many years of his life working in South Africa standing up for those who were treated badly by **apartheid**.

As a Christian he was against those who were not white being treated differently, and he felt it was wrong to do nothing about it.

Huddleston led the British movement against apartheid. He encouraged people around the world to refuse to play South African teams in sports events and also not to buy South African goods, such as wine.

He became friends with other people involved in the anti-apartheid movement such as **Nelson Mandela**.

Before he died in 1998, Trevor Huddleston saw the system of apartheid ended.

Case study: RAY DAVEY

In 2007 Ray Davey celebrated his 90th birthday. But who is he? What has he done to fight prejudice in Northern Ireland?

In 1964 Ray Davey was involved in setting up a new Christian community called Corrymeela. The community wanted to show that people of different traditions can work together, learn about and respect one another.

A residential centre in Ballycastle, Co Antrim was purchased in 1965. Today the Corrymeela community works with schools, families, senior citizens, community groups and churches both in Northern Ireland and beyond.

Find out more about Corrymeela at www.corrymeela.org

The photograph is from the Cain Web Service (Background on the Northern Ireland Conflict): cain.ulst.ac.uk

Jesus' miracles

What is a miracle?

A miracle is something that does not usually happen.
But is it more than this?

A miracle is when the impossible happens.
But is it more than this?

When Jesus was alive he performed many miracles.

The miracles he did can be sorted into four different types.

1. Healing the sick
2. Controlling nature
3. Removing demons
4. Raising the dead to life

Com TPD WO

Write down your own definition of a miracle.

Compare your definition with others written by your classmates.

Has anyone written down a different definition to yours?

Put all of your ideas together and come up with a class definition of a miracle.

TPD

Look at the following headlines. Do you think any of them are miraculous?

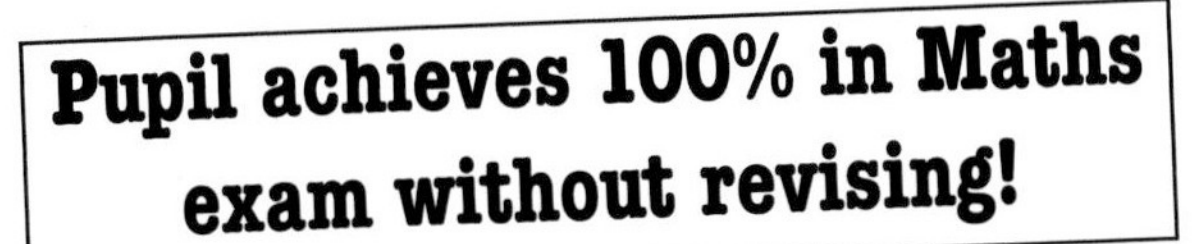

Woman survives plane crash in which all other passengers died.

Girl's headache cured after taking a headache tablet.

Boy has sprained ankle after falling from sixth floor window.

Woman recovers from cancer – doctors are amazed.

Man regains consciousness after one year in a coma.

Jesus' power over death

TPD
SM
PD

I'm afraid of...

Decide if you are afraid of any of the things below. Rate each one with a number from 0-10, with 0 = "not at all afraid" and 10 = "scared stiff".

Add in any other things that you are afraid of.

How many of you gave fear of death ten points?
If you ranked death highly, can you explain why?
Some of you may not have given it a high rating.
If so, why are you not so afraid of it?

People are afraid of many different things. Some people's fear is so intense, they are said to have a phobia. Do you recognise any of them?

Acrophobia	fear of heights
Agoraphobia	fear of open spaces
Botanophobia	fear of plants
Ergophobia	fear of work
Phobophobia	fear of being afraid
Claustrophobia	fear of enclosed spaces
Zoophobia	fear of animals

MI

Select a newspaper and count the number of references to death in it.

It's possible to see a lot of deaths on our televisions, whether they are real or just in stories.

Do you think we have become hardened to the sight of death?

TPD

Some people are so afraid of death that they don't like using the word and instead use other words or phrases.

Can you think of any of the words or phrases people use instead of the word 'death'?

TPD
PD

Read these quotations and discuss what you think each one means.

"Death devours lambs as well as sheep."

"It is a poor thing for anyone to fear that which is inevitable."

"A faithful Christian life in this world is the best preparation for the next."

"The final heartbeat for the Christian is not the mysterious conclusion to a meaningless existence. It is rather, the grand beginning to a life that will never end."

JESUS RAISES LAZARUS FROM THE DEAD

One thing all of us can say for certain is that eventually we will die. You may think that this is very sad, but we cannot avoid it. It happens to everyone.

However, by this miracle Jesus wanted to show that death is not the end.

Read the story in John 11:1-44

John 11:35 – "Jesus wept".

The shortest verse in the New Testament.

BC
TPD
WO

Imagine that it is one week since Lazarus was raised from the dead.

In pairs, write an imaginary interview with him. Think about the questions you would ask and the answers he might give.

You could perform your interview for the rest of your class.

TPD

What do you think these words mean?

"I am the resurrection and the life."

John 11:25

BC

Design a poster to illustrate John 11:25.

BETHANY TIMES

Daily Edition

Today our small town was thrown into uproar by a terrifying, yet miraculous event. A man by the name of Lazarus, the brother of Martha and Mary, walked from his tomb four days after his burial. Residents reported that Lazarus had died after suffering a serious illness.

Eyewitnesses to these astonishing events report that a man named Jesus of Nazareth, a close friend of the family, was present when Lazarus rose from the dead.

This Jesus has made the headlines many times in recent months because of his power to heal sickness and cast out demons.

Many who were present when Lazarus appeared from the tomb believe that it was the authority of Jesus that made it happen.

According to a member of Lazarus' family, the sisters had sent word to Jesus, informing him of their brother's illness. However, he had been engaged in teaching in another part of the country and had not made it to Bethany in time to save their brother.

On arrival in the town, Jesus went straight to the tomb of Lazarus and ordered the stone in front of it to be rolled away. He then shouted into the tomb, "Lazarus, come out!" It was at this point that Lazarus walked out, still wrapped in his burial clothes.

A local person who was present stated that she was terrified and could only watch in amazement. Jesus ordered that Lazarus be unwrapped and they all returned to the family home.

It is anticipated that this event will help to increase Jesus' popularity with the people.

MI
TPD

1 What was the family connection between Mary, Martha and Lazarus?
2 What message did the sisters send to Jesus?
3 Why do you think Jesus did not go to Lazarus straight away?
4 How long had Lazarus been buried when Jesus visited the tomb?
5 What do you think Jesus was trying to prove to the people who saw this miracle?
6 Are there things about this miracle that puzzle you?
7 If you could ask these people questions, what would you ask? Who would you ask?

Com
BC

Pretend that you are the journalist who wrote the report above.
Think of a headline for it. Remember it must be suitable for a newspaper.

JESUS HEALS JAIRUS' DAUGHTER

Read the story in Mark 5:21-43.

MI
TPD

Here is a code. Work it out and complete it.

A=Z; B=Y; C=X; D=W; etc.

Now use the code to work out this message:

QZRIFH DZH ZM LUURXRZO RM GSV HBMZTLTFV.

SRH WZFTSGVI DZH ROO ZMW SV ZHPVW QVHFH GL SVZO SVI.

BC
WO

In groups, make a drama presentation of this story.

Com
BC
WO

Working in pairs, imagine that one of you witnessed the raising of Jairus' daughter.

Sitting back to back with your partner, imagine you are on the phone to a friend. They find your story hard to believe.

You have to convince the other person that it really happened.

TPD

Do you think this miracle proves anything about Jesus?

Explain your answer.

Jesus' power over demons

JESUS HEALS A MAN WITH A LEGION OF EVIL SPIRITS

Read Mark 5:1-20. Now perform this imaginary role-play.

Narrator 1: This miracle occurred on the shores of Lake Galilee. Jesus and the disciples had just moored the boat when a man called Legion approached them, shouting at the top of his voice…

Legion: Jesus, Son of God, do not punish me, I beg you.

Narrator 2 The disciples crowded around Jesus to get a better look at this very strange man. He was dirty, with long uncombed hair and a straggly beard.

Disciple 1: Who is he? Look at the rags he is wearing. Does he actually live here amongst the burial tombs?

Disciple 2: Yes, I have heard about him. His name is Legion and he is demon-possessed. People have tried to chain him down, but he has great strength and he breaks the irons they put on his feet.

Narrator 1: As they were talking, Legion continued to shout and babble in a loud, piercing voice. Suddenly Legion lunged towards Jesus and fell on his knees before him. He screamed out again ….

Legion: Jesus, Son of the Most High God. What do you want with me? For God's sake I beg you, don't punish me!

Narrator 2: Jesus knew that Legion was possessed by an evil spirit and it was the spirit that was talking, so he said …

Jesus: Evil spirit, come out of this man.

Narrator 1: The evil spirits begged Jesus not to destroy them, but Jesus ordered them to leave the man and enter a herd of pigs that were grazing nearby. Immediately the entire herd of 2000 pigs rushed down the side of the hill and were drowned in the lake.

Narrator 2: The pig herder rushed off to tell everyone what had happened. When the people came to see, they were amazed to find Legion sitting quietly and in his right mind.

Legion: I am so grateful to you, Jesus. Look what you have done for me. Please let me go with you.

Jesus: No, Legion, go back to your home and

family and tell them how much the Lord has done for you and how kind he has been to you.

Narrator 1: Legion went around telling his story and all who heard it were amazed.

BC

Design a cartoon strip to retell the story of Jesus healing Legion.

TPD

What do you think of this miracle?

Is there anything you wonder about?

TPD PD

Do evil spirits exist today?

Many Christians believe that they do, but that Jesus has defeated them.

Many people accept that there is evil in the world but they find it difficult to accept evil spirits.

What do you think?

Jesus' power over disease

THE PARALYSED MAN

Read Mark 2:1–12.

Jesus was in Capernaum and news spread that he was there. So many people gathered to hear him that the house he was visiting was full. There was nowhere to stand, not even outside the door.

As Jesus was teaching, some people came carrying a paralysed man. Four of the men carried the man onto the roof of the house. They made a hole in the roof and lowered their friend down in front of Jesus.

Jesus saw that these men had great faith, so he said to the paralysed man, "Your sins are forgiven".

Some of the religious leaders saw this and they started to criticise Jesus. They said, "Why does he say things like that? He is speaking against God because only God has the power to forgive sins".

Jesus knew what they were thinking, so he said to them, "Why do you say such things? Is it easier to forgive a man's sins or to make him walk? I will prove to you that I have the authority to forgive sins."

Jesus told the paralysed man to pick up his mat and go home. Immediately the man obeyed and everyone who saw this was amazed.

TPD

In Bible times people believed that sickness was the result of sin. If you were paralysed, like this man, then either you or your parents were thought to be guilty of some dreadful sin.

Think about this: Why does Jesus say that if he is able to heal the man, he will have proved that he can forgive his sins as well?

Com BC TPD

1 Write down four words that describe how this man may have felt once he was healed.

2 Pretend that you are the paralysed man. Write a postcard to your family, telling them what has happened to you.

3 Imagine you are the owner of the house where this miracle occurred. Give an account of what happened and how you feel about it. Think about everything that happened!

ICT MI BC

Use the internet to find out about Joni Eareckson Tada who was paralysed in a diving accident when she was just 17 years old.

Find a picture of her if you can. Wordprocess a page of information about her.

Jesus' power over nature

TPD
BC

Have you ever been on a boat during a storm or when the sea was really rough? Was it a big boat, like a ship?

Can you imagine how afraid the disciples were when they were in a really small boat in a fierce storm on the Sea of Galilee?

Sudden storms still blow down from the hills onto it.

JESUS CALMS THE STORM ON THE SEA OF GALILEE

Here is an imaginary account of what happened.

The disciples were just exhausted.

All day crowds and crowds of people had been following Jesus, listening as he taught and watching as he healed the sick. Now the sun was beginning to set over the Sea of Galilee.

Seeing how tired his disciples were, Jesus said, "Let's get in a boat and go over to the other side of the lake". It would be good for all of them to get away from the crowds for a while.

iStockphoto/Tim Kimberley

Sudden storms still blow down from the hills onto the Sea of Galilee.

The disciples rowed away from the shore while Jesus went to the back of the boat and lay down on a cushion. The waves lapped gently against the side of the boat, lulling Jesus into a peaceful sleep.

But suddenly a wind began to blow dark clouds across the sky. The waves weren't so gentle any more. The little boat began to pitch and rock. The disciples began to get a little worried.

But Jesus still lay sleeping in the back of the boat.

Then the wind grew stronger still. The spray from the waves got the disciples all wet. This was turning into a bad storm! But Jesus still lay sleeping in the back of the boat.

By the time the fishing boat reached the centre of the lake, the wind had turned into an angry gale that whipped the waves so high they washed right over the boat. The disciples were terrified. They thought they might drown. But Jesus still lay sleeping.

Finally, one of the disciples went and shook Jesus. "Master," he cried, "don't you care if we drown?" Jesus looked around. He listened to the howling wind. He felt the cold, stinging spray as waves crashed over the little boat. He saw the fear in the faces of his disciples.

Then Jesus stood, stretched out his arms to the wind and the waves, and commanded: "Peace! Be still!" All at once the wind died down and the waves became completely calm.

Then he asked the disciples: "Why are you so afraid? Where is your faith?"

The disciples were amazed and asked each other, "Who is this man? Even the wind and waves obey him!"

MI

TPD

Now read Mark 4: 35-41.

Compare Mark's account with the imaginary account.

What is the same?

What is different?

Which one do you think is most likely to be true?

Why?

TPD

Why do you think Jesus performed miracles?

Remember that there can be more than one reason for something.

DO MIRACLES HAPPEN TODAY?

Read this story which is by a real person.

My story begins back in Easter 2003, when I was admitted to Craigavon Area Hospital with suspected appendicitis. However, investigations revealed what they took to be a large cyst on my kidney and arrangements were made for me to stay for a couple of days in hospital in August to drain the cyst – a relatively simple and routine procedure.

We moved to Newcastle, County Down, at the beginning of July, where my husband William, a Methodist minister, was settling into his new circuit of three churches, and the family into their new home and schools. I checked into the hospital at the end of August, but the expected procedure hadn't worked as hoped, and the scans revealed that it was not a cyst on my kidney, but a large **tumour**.

The decision was taken that I should have major surgery to remove the tumour, followed by a few tests to prove that it was **benign**. The tumour had turned out to be extremely rare. Various test were done and finally we got the news that the tumour contained malignant cancer cells.

My scan took place on 27 January, and shortly afterwards my consultant told me that it had shown up **lesions** on my kidneys and that I would have to come back into hospital after three months.

I was admitted to hospital at the end of April, hoping that my scans would reveal better news, but it was not to be. As my consultant came into the room I knew by the look on his face that things were not good. "Unfortunately lesions have now appeared on your lungs", he said. "If they turn out to be secondaries, then it will lead to your death."

It was all a blur; I was to be referred to a specialist cancer consultant in Belvoir Park hospital, but there was no hope here.

So, on the first of May, through the tears, I took my first step of faith. I opened up a red notebook that William handed to me and wrote across the top of the first page: "By his stripes I am healed – My Story of how God healed me". I began a daily journal, recording the feelings and emotions that I had, and the way in which the Lord spoke to me as I started to claim the healing verses from his Word every day. We started to read Psalm 91 together every morning and every evening – it became a part of my life.

Further scans were arranged over the next few weeks. The MRI scan was at 8.00 am, an early start from Newcastle, and we played a song called "The Voice of Hope" over and over again on the way to the hospital.

We didn't expect to have another consultation until July, but I was called back on Monday for the results. That was 21 June – well named "the longest day". The consultant explained that there was a large tumour on my right lung, while further lesions had appeared on both lungs also.

The cancer was inoperable and treatment was unlikely to work. If it did, it would only add a matter of weeks to my life. I asked him how long I would have, and he said, "A year at the most, possibly less than that depending on how aggressively it is progressing".

I just collapsed into William's arms – I knew the news would not be good, but I had no idea that it would be quite this bad.

We drove back to Newcastle to face the family. That was the most difficult part – how do you tell your mother and your teenagers that you have less than a year to live? But still I was claiming my healing by faith in God's word, and standing on some words which I received "Jesus is the name above all names – cancer is only a name – and Jesus' name is above cancer".

With no operation or treatment available, either the Lord moved miraculously, or I would be dead within the year, as the doctors had said. We determined to go wherever the Lord would lead us for prayer.

We went to friends in Cardiff where we spent a Saturday evening receiving ministry, then on the Tuesday evening to 'The Ministry of Power' meeting at Renewal in Solihull, where we met Pastor Dave Carr, and had a wonderful sense that by the end of this time, the cancer had left my body, and I was healed.

We travelled home and I had all the scans and waited for the results, all the while claiming God's healing promises for my life.

On Friday 9 July, we met my consultant in his office in Craigavon hospital, where he greeted me with the words, "Sharyn, you are going to leave this hospital a happier girl than you came in today!"

He was about to start going through a very large medical file when I said, "Just tell me – am I going to die?"

"No!" he said, with an even broader smile, "not that I know of anyway!"

William hugged me with delight, we both knew that God had done it!

The file showed that three world authorities had examined the tumour and confirmed the cancer. The purpose for this meeting had been to check the progression of the tumours, and from that see how long I had left to live – perhaps even less than the year that had been suggested, depending on how aggressive it was. The most recent scans showed no trace of cancer at all! We left the hospital with such joy – God had been faithful to his Word!

Since then we have been amazed at the stories we have heard of God's healing power through our ministry, which we have moved into full time since January 2006.

Interviews have followed in the media, on UTV, BBC Radio and TV's Stephen Nolan Show, UCB, and among other printed media *The Daily Mirror* and *Woman's Own* magazine.

www.longlifeministries.org

Jesus' Teachings

Forgiveness

TPD
PD

What does it mean to forgive? Read the following comments on forgiveness.

Forgiveness is wiping the slate clean.
H Chambers

To forgive is to maintain a relationship with someone despite the hurt you feel they have done you. The hurt does in some sense remain there, but healed or transformed in the context of a continuing relationship.
Richard Harries

In the Bible, God's forgiveness is described as trampling our sins underfoot and throwing them into the depths of the sea.
see Micah 7:19

The weak can never forgive. Forgiveness is the attribute of the strong.
Mahatma Gandhi

Now write your own definition.

TPD
PD

Are some things unforgivable?

Decide where the following wrongdoings fall on the forgiveness scale.

Think carefully before deciding and give reasons for your choices.

FORGIVABLE		UNFORGIVABLE
1 2 3 4	5 6	7 8 9 10

Someone you don't know very well steals from you.

Your best friend steals money from your blazer.

A drunk driver crashes his car and kills a member of your family.

Terrorist attacks like September 11 2001 or the London bombings.

One of your close friends goes out with your boy/girl friend behind your back.

You have planned to go to a club that your parents have warned you not to go to because there are drug dealers there. Your friend has agreed to cover for you, but at the last minute tells their own parents what is happening. Your parents find out and you are in big trouble.

TPD
PD

Why do you think it is difficult to forgive people when they hurt us? Write down two reasons.

It may be difficult to forgive ...

It may be difficult to forgive ...

TPD

SIX-YEAR-OLD DEAD

Parents forgive drunk driver

A clergyman and his wife have forgiven the drunk driver who killed their son. The young boy's father, Reverend Michael Counsell said:

"We had to forgive the driver because every day we say the Lord's Prayer and we would choke on it if we were not forgiving. Forgiveness is a form of love."

Michael and Elaine Counsell felt that they had to forgive. What reasons did they give?

Read this role-play on forgiveness.

Narrator: The following incident took place in the middle of the Spanish Civil War in which villages were set on fire. When one troop of National soldiers had cleared a village of their opponents (the Red Army) they found in a corner, a badly wounded Red Army soldier, his chest pierced by a splinter from a grenade. With glazed eyes the wounded man watched the approaching patrol. Then he feebly raised a hand and stammered:

Red Army Soldier: A priest! Get me a priest.

Narrator: The soldiers found a priest and brought him to the soldier.

Priest: You want to confess?

Red Army Soldier: Yes, I want to confess. But tell me, are you the priest of this village?

Priest: Yes I am.

Narrator: It was a long time before the priest left the dying man. His hair was soaked with sweat and his face white as he returned to the waiting patrol.

Priest: Take the wounded man into that house, so he does not die in the street.

Narrator: When the soldiers approached the young man, he raised himself and sighed to them.

Red Army Soldier: He forgave me! How can he have done this?

National Soldier: Why shouldn't he forgive you? That's his business.

Red Army Soldier: You don't understand what I have done. On my own I killed thirty-two priests; I stabbed, shot, struck down, throttled. In every village I made it my business to arrive first at the house of the priest and I did the same here. The priest was not in, but I found his father and two brothers. I asked them where the priest was, but they refused to betray him. So I shot all three. Do you understand? I killed his father and brothers, yet he forgave me.

Pierre Lefevre,
One Hundred Stories to Change Your Life
(Pauline Books & Media, 1991)

JESUS' TEACHING ON FORGIVENESS

TPD
SM
PD

Have you ever done something that you had to say sorry for?

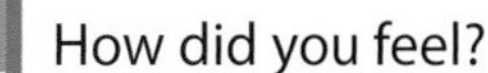

How did you feel?

Were you *really* sorry?

How would you know if you were?

Christians believe that before they can enter the Kingdom of God each of them must ask God to forgive their sins. They must tell God that they are sorry for the wrong they have done. This is called **repentance**.

However, this is not the end of Jesus' teaching on forgiveness. He made it clear that if people want God to forgive them, they must be willing to forgive other people who hurt them.

Jesus told the parable of the unforgiving servant in order to illustrate what he meant. Read the parable in Matthew 18:21-35.

TPD

Talk about this story. What do you think Jesus is saying in it?

MI BC

Imagine you are the servant who reported what the ungrateful man had done.

Write down the exact words you would say to the master. Remember you are indignant and want to see fair play.

MI BC Cit PD

Do you know what a 'moral dilemma' is? If not, find out.

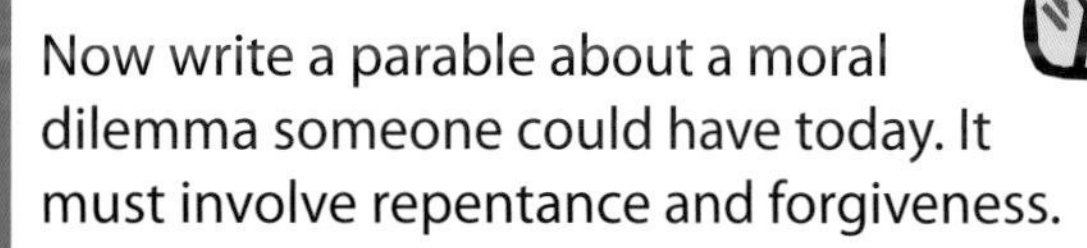

Now write a parable about a moral dilemma someone could have today. It must involve repentance and forgiveness.

Com TPD WO

"It is possible to practice unlimited forgiveness in the 21st century."

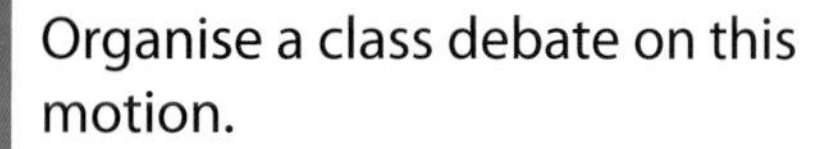

Organise a class debate on this motion.

BC TPD

1 See who can be the first to make ten or more words out of the word 'forgiveness'.

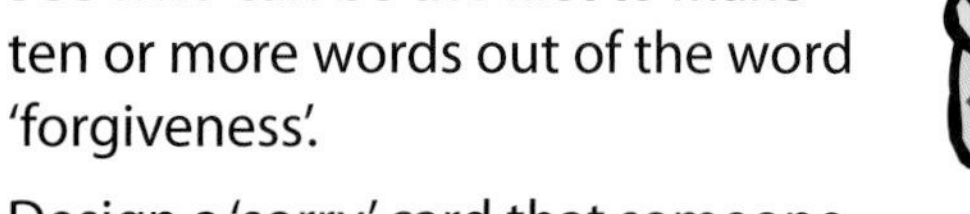

2 Design a 'sorry' card that someone could use to apologise for something.

3 Write a prayer of repentance.

Judgement

TPD

What do you see in this picture?

What is going on?

TPD Cit

What does the word authority mean?

What sorts of authority do you come across?

For Christians, the person with the greatest authority over them is God.

MI

What does the word 'respect' mean?

MI TPD PD

Find newspaper articles which show people's lack of respect for authority.

Talk about them and answer these questions.

How can lack of authority be shown?

How can lack of respect be shown?

TPD
Cit

Passing judgement

What would you do in the following situations?

Discuss them with your partner and record a verdict.

iStockphoto/Lise Gagne

Case number 1:

Michael is a 27 year old nurse. He caused £400 worth of criminal damage to a car after a night out with friends. He claims he had been drinking and was on medication and that the combination had affected his behaviour. Michael told the court he was sorry for his actions.

iStockphoto/Anne Clark

Case number 2:

Sarah, a 23 year old single mother forged two job references in order to get a job as a shop assistant. She has no previous convictions. She told the court that she needed the money for Christmas.

iStockphoto/judy picciotto

Case number 3:

Lynda is 33 years old and has admitted leaving a fire bomb in a ladies' fashion store. The court was told a member of staff spotted Lynda acting suspiciously near the show display. The discovery of the fire bomb caused major disruption to adjoining businesses and shoppers during the town summer festival.

iStockphoto/Gabriel Moisa

Case number 4:

Peter, a 19 year old student was doing a favour for a friend when he was stopped by police and found to be driving without a licence or the supervision of a qualified driver. This was the second time he had been before the court for the same offences.

Possible Verdicts

1 One hundred hours community service

2 A £50 fine

3 A conditional discharge (This means the person is let off with a warning not to commit the offence again within a certain time.)

4 Six months' imprisonment suspended for 2 years

5 A conditional discharge with an order to pay compensation

There are 21 courthouses in Northern Ireland.

The headquarters is in Belfast.

You can find out more about the court service of Northern Ireland from their web site www.courtsni.gov.uk

The courthouse in Downpatrick

JESUS AND JUDGEMENT

The Jews thought that the Messiah would come at the end of time to set up a new heaven and earth.

The disciples thought that Jesus was the Messiah, so they asked him about things that would happen at 'the end of the age'.

MI TPD PD

Read Matthew 24:1-35

Now write down some of the signs of Jesus' return.

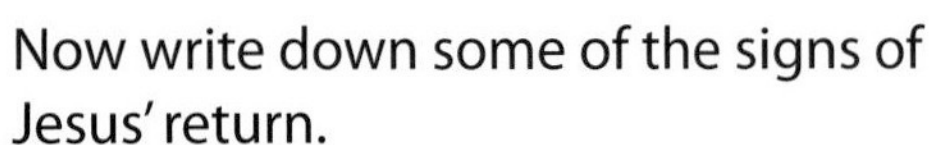

Talk about these. Decide which you think would be worst.

Are there any you wouldn't worry about at all?

TPD SM

If you heard that Jesus was coming back next week, would you do anything different?

TPD SM WO

How would you spend your last week on earth?

Write down an answer to this question.

Now divide into groups and compare your answers.

What is the same about them all?

What is different?

Jesus taught a great deal about the Kingdom of God. It will be a time of peace and blessing on earth when evil will be judged and suffering will end.

The Parable of the Sheep and the Goats

Christians believe that after death God will use his authority to judge people according to how they have lived.

Jesus' teaching about the Day of Judgement can be found in the parable of the sheep and the goats.

The parable refers to the Judgement at the great white throne at the end of the age.

God will divide people into 2 groups:

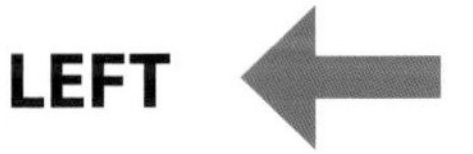

RIGHT

Christians believe that on the Day of Judgement God will decide who he will allow into his kingdom, and who will not be allowed in.

The judgement will be based on how people have behaved during their lives.

MI TPD

Read Matthew 25:31-46.

How does this passage say that God makes his decisions about people?

What words would you use to describe people who went to the left?

What words would you use to describe people who went to the right?

JUDGED SUCCESSFUL

To be successful in a job application you have to have the qualifications the employer wants.

For example you need to have a HGV driving licence to drive lorry. You might need a health and hygiene certificate to be a kitchen assistant or the ECDL qualification to work in an office.

MI

The Gospels contain other criteria which will be used for judgement.

Look up the following passages and make a note of what they say:

1 Matthew 10:22
2 Mark 16:16
3 Luke 23:39-43
4 John 3:16-17

BEING PREPARED FOR JUDGEMENT

BC
TPD
WO

Read Matthew 25:1-13 'The Ten Bridesmaids' (or 'virgins')

What do you think this story is about?

In groups, imagine Jesus is telling this story today. What example might he use instead of bridesmaids?

Write a role-play of your ideas and then perform them for the class.

TPD
BC
WO

Imagine you are one of the Bridesmaids.

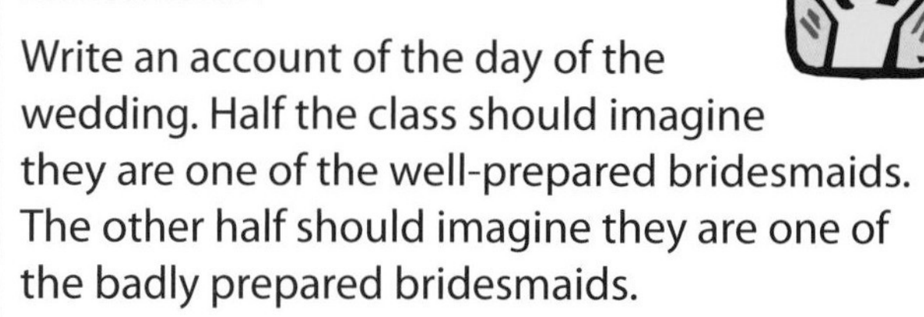

Write an account of the day of the wedding. Half the class should imagine they are one of the well-prepared bridesmaids. The other half should imagine they are one of the badly prepared bridesmaids.

Compare the accounts. What do you notice?

Is there one point where a mistake was made?

THE RESULTS OF JUDGEMENT

The rich man and Lazarus

To show how rich this man was, Jesus said he "dressed in purple and fine linen." (Luke 16:19-31)

Purple clothing was associated with the very rich because the dye to make it was very expensive. Purple dye was extracted from a rare shellfish.

The rich man dressed in the most expensive clothing available during his time. Every day he lived a life of great luxury.

In all the parables of Jesus, Lazarus is the only character who is given a proper name. His name means 'God has helped'.

Lazarus is really poor compared to the rich man. He was also in a lot of pain all the time.

The only pain relief he got was from the dogs who licked his sores.

In the first century Jews thought of dogs as unclean animals.

Lazarus lay at the rich man's gate, longing to be fed by the crumbs that fell from the rich man's table.

MI

Read the story in Luke 16:19-31.

Now close your Bible and say if these statements are true or false.

1 The rich man was nice to Lazarus when they were alive.
2 The rich man was worried about his brothers.
3 The rich man's brothers did not know about God.
4 The rich man's importance on earth made him important after death.
5 Lazarus suffered on earth because he was a sinner.

TPD
SM

Trading places

The rich man and Lazarus swopped places in the end!

Is there any one you would like to swop places with? Why or why not?

What would be good about swopping places? What would be bad about swopping places?

THE TEACHING OF THE EARLY CHURCH

The topic of judgement made up part of the preaching of the early church.

2 Peter 2:9

2 Timothy 4:8

Hebrews 9:27

ICT
BC

Make a collage

1 In the Middle Ages very few people could read. As well as preaching to them about judgement, the priests often had pictures painted on the walls of the church to frighten their listeners. The priests wanted people to lead good lives.

Make a collage representing judgement.

Use newspapers, magazines, artwork, books and the internet to help you.

2 A famous sculptor and painter called Michaelangelo painted a picture of the Last Judgement.

Find out as much as you can about it and write a report.

Organise your report under headings and present it in an envelope or folder to your teacher.

LOVE

In this unit you are going to explore what love means in action and what the Bible has to say to Christians about it.

TPD

In pairs, write down a definition of 'love'.

Is it difficult?

One problem with the word 'love', as you have probably just discovered, is that we use it to mean many different things.

TPD

Write down five things that you love.

Each sentence should begin 'I love. . .'

MI
BC

The love game

Everyone has to say something they love. Do it this way.

Start: I love chocolate.

The next person has to use the last letter of chocolate which is 'e' and say that they love something beginning with the letter 'e'. The third person then uses the last letter of *that* word so on until the whole class has taken part.

Challenge: Can your class complete this in three minutes? What about two minutes?

The Greeks have four different words for love.

1 **Philos** – this is the kind of love we have for our closest friends.

2 **Storge** – is sentimental love for animals, objects and so on.

BC
PD

Draw some pictures of things which you feel sentimental about and underneath write an explanation.

3 **Eros** – is the romantic love which people have for each other.

Christians follow the teaching of God in Genesis where he said that men and women should marry and share a special love together.

4 **Agape** – is Christian love which is self sacrificing love.

It is the kind of love shown by the Good Samaritan who helped the injured man even at personal cost. It is also the kind of love Christians believe Jesus showed by dying on the cross. Mother Teresa showed 'Agape' love towards the people she worked amongst in Calcutta. She sacrificed all of the comforts and luxuries of life to help others. You can read about her on page 71 of Book 2.

BC

Draw a cross and write the words of John 3:16 inside it.

BC
WO

Working in groups, produce a poster using the four different Greek words for love.

Decide how you will go about this.

What do you need to do first?

TPD

How many films based on a love story can your class name?

What have all these films in common? Do you notice any differences?

Do they always end happily?

VALENTINE'S DAY

TPD

Do you think sending Valentine cards is a good idea?

Where did the idea of Valentine's day come from?

The name 'valentine' comes from a Latin word 'valour' which means 'worthy'. So you send cards to show how worthy someone is!

Today the Catholic Church remembers at least three saints with the name 'Valentine' or 'Valentinus'. The church remembers them all on 14th February.

According to one legend, Valentine was a priest in Rome during the third century. The Emperor Claudius decided that single soldiers were better than married ones and so he banned marriage for them.

Valentine thought that this wasn't fair and so he defied Claudius and performed marriages for soldiers in secret.

Saint Valentine

When Claudius discovered what Valentine had been doing, he ordered that he should be put to death.

Valentine is supposed to have sent a friend a card 'From your Valentine' before his execution and this started the custom of exchanging messages of love.

Other stories say that Valentine may have been helping Christians escape Roman prisons where they were often tortured and beaten, and was killed for doing this.

BC

Design a Valentine's day card.

What images could you use?

PROBLEMS IN LOVE

TPD
PD

Problems In Love

Read the following problems. Discuss with a partner what you think the solution could be.

Problem 1: **Am I ugly?**

I'm feeling pretty rotten. My girlfriend dumped me because she thinks I'm ugly. She shouted it across the classroom yesterday in French. Everybody heard her, even the teacher.

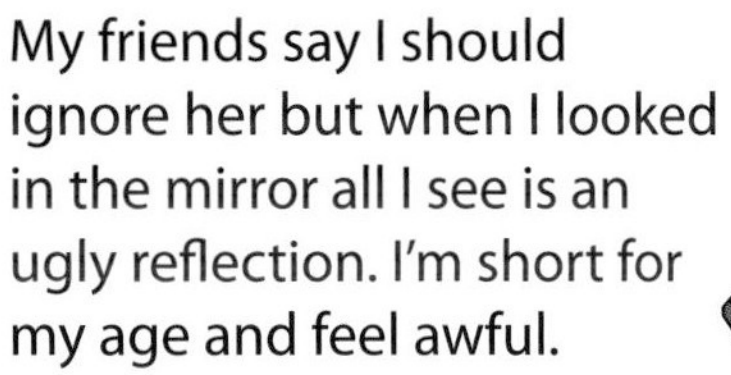

My friends say I should ignore her but when I looked in the mirror all I see is an ugly reflection. I'm short for my age and feel awful.

I hate the way I look and the way I feel. What can I do?

Problem 2: **We fight all the time**

I have been going out with my boyfriend for a year now. The problem is we keep fighting. I always moan at him and I don't feel I can trust him around other girls.

Sometimes we split up for a while. We always end up in some sort of argument, usually over something pointless.

At the moment we're not together as we fought and he hit me.

I love him but should I bother trying to get him back?

WHAT DOES THE BIBLE SAY ABOUT LOVE OR CHRISTIAN LOVE?

A well known description of love in the New Testament comes from Paul.

Paul wrote letters to the Christians living in Corinth because he wanted them to live together in peace.

The Corinthians were behaving badly. Some of them thought they were more important than others. Some of them envied what others had. So Paul wrote in his first letter to them about what true love is.

ICT
MI
BC
TPD
PD

Read 1 Corinthians 13:4-8.

Compare what Paul says love is with your own definitions of love.

Is there more to it than you thought?

Design a wall poster around these verses. You could use a computer and illustrations.

In other words, Christians should love one another, the way God loves them.

MI
TPD
SM
Cit
PD

Find out what promises a couple takes when they are getting married.

What do you think of these promises? Could you keep them? Are they difficult?

In your own words, make up promises that you think could be said at a marriage.

Jesus showed how much God loves people through three parables:

The Lost Sheep

The Lost Coin

The Lost Son

Each story makes the same point – God loves people no matter who they are.

The parable of the lost sheep

Many people at the time of Jesus worked as farmers. Their livestock, often sheep, were very important to them.

Read Matthew 8:10-14.

Jesus told a story about a man who had one hundred sheep but lost one of them. He left the other 99 and searched high and low for his missing sheep.

MI

Copy out these sentences and fill in the gaps.

Imagine that you owned one hundred sheep. One day, when you count them _______ is missing.

You don't stop for a moment, but leave the other ninety-_______ in the field and set off to look for the one _________ sheep.

And when you find it, you are absolutely __________. You put it on your _________ and hurry back to the rest. You tell everyone the good news and invite your _____________ and _____________ in to share in your happiness.

The parable of the lost coin

Read Luke 16:8-10.

A lady had ten silver coins but she lost one and so she swept the house looking for it until she found it.

TPD

Memory game

Put ten things on a desk where everyone can see them.

Now everyone must close their eyes while one person removes something. Who is first to say what's missing?

Christians believe that no matter how many people there are in the world, God notices and cares about everyone of them – not just ten!

SM
PD

Have you ever lost something really, really important?

If you would like to, tell the class all about it.

Did you find it?

The parable of the prodigal son

Read this modern day version of the parable of the prodigal son

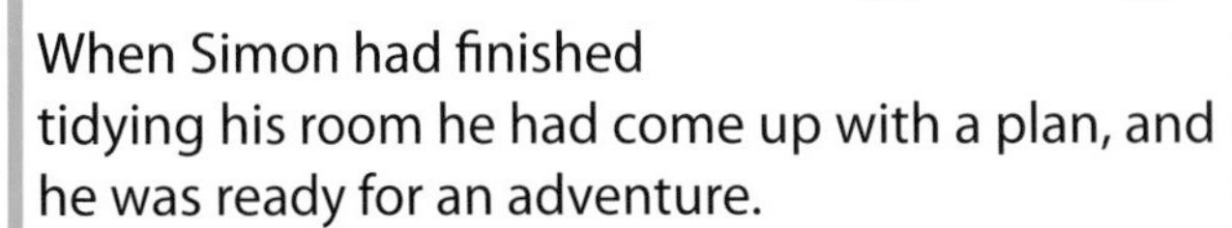

"Simon do this, Simon do that. Why do I always have to do all the work?" Simon grumbled as he tidied his room. He had already been to the local shop for milk and had walked the dog whilst his sister continued to surf the net. "I never get to do the things I want to do when I want to do them."

When Simon had finished tidying his room he had come up with a plan, and he was ready for an adventure.

He crept into the kitchen and sneaked quietly out the back door, thinking no one would notice he had gone. He went to the bottom of the garden and climbed the fence. Then he wandered along the path to Castle woods and finally came to a clearing near the Drumkeen river, which was one of the favourite secret spots belonging to him and his friends.

"A-H-H-H, this is just *great*!" he thought. "Now I can do anything I want to do and nobody can make me work. I'll just stay here and have *fun, fun, fun*."

He watched spiders crawl over a rock and tried to block their path with a stick. He threw stones into the water trying to get them to bounce.

After getting tired of that game, he pulled his MP3 player out of his pocket. How wonderful he felt being free from his mother's nagging!

Simon started to get tired, and it seemed to be getting darker. He decided to lie down on the grass and rest. It was nice for little while, but then it became uncomfortable. No matter how he turned, the ground was hard and he didn't have a pillow or a blanket.

Then he heard his stomach growling. "I'm getting *really hungry*," he said. But there wasn't anything to munch. "Why didn't I think to bring food?"

The woods were becoming darker and darker. He was getting hungrier and hungrier. Then he heard a strange screeching noise followed by a snapping of branches. "What was *that*?" he thought, scared.

"I know what I'll do. I'll just have to go back home. I'll sneak in. Mum always has crisps in the cupboard and some fizzy drink in the fridge. I'll scrounge a few packets and eat them lying on my bed watching TV. No one will ever know I've been gone. Happy days."

Really scared, he ran out of the woods down the path towards his house. He had never thought about how spooky the woods could be at night when you were on your own.

As Simon ran, he thought, "Will I be able to get into the house without any fuss?"
"I wonder if they missed me?"

"I wonder will I get told off?"

Slowly he climbed over the fence trying not to rip his T-shirt. The security light came on lighting up the whole garden. "Oh nightmare! They'll know now that I'm outside."

Then he heard voices. "There he is! There he is!"

His father ran down the steps and asked him where he had been. His mother met them at the kitchen door and hugged him. She was glad he was safe. Sarah, his little sister was squealing and jumping around pleased.

It was all too much for Simon but they just wanted him to know they loved him.

Now read Luke's account of how Jesus told it. You will find it in Luke 15:11-32.

MI
WO

Divide into teams. One person will be the writer. Your teacher will call out these questions. See which team gets the most right answers.

Close your books now!

1 How many sons did the man have?

a. 4 b. 6 c. 2

2 What did the son ask his father to give him?

a. a limousine
b. a pedigree cow
c. his inheritance

3 Which son left home?

a. the middle son
b. the younger son
c. the elder son

4 What did he do with the money?

a. put it in a savings account
b. burned it for heat
c. spent it

5 What kind of job did he get?

a. feeding pigs
b. shop assistant
c. bus driver

6 Why did he decide to go back home?

a. he was missing his favourite TV programmes
b. he was starving
c. he loved his family

7 How did his father react when he returned home?

a. told him to get a job
b. ignored him
c. kissed and hugged him

TPD

1 Imagine you are the father in this story. Why might you give your younger son what he asked for? Are there any reasons why it mightn't be a good idea to give him this?

2 Do you understand how the older son felt when his brother came back? Explain how he felt in your own words.

3 What do you think Jesus is teaching in this story?

BC

Choose one of the characters in the story – the father, the younger son or the older brother.

Write three diary entries for your character: one at the time the younger son leaves; one while he is away; one when he returns.

BC

Write a roleplay of the scene where the older brother reacts to his brother's return.

Com
MI
BC

Imagine you are a news reporter on the local paper and have just heard about a family welcoming home a penniless son who had left some time ago taking a family fortune with him.

One of the servants has been useful in telling you what happened when the son returned.

Organise your news article like the pyramid below.

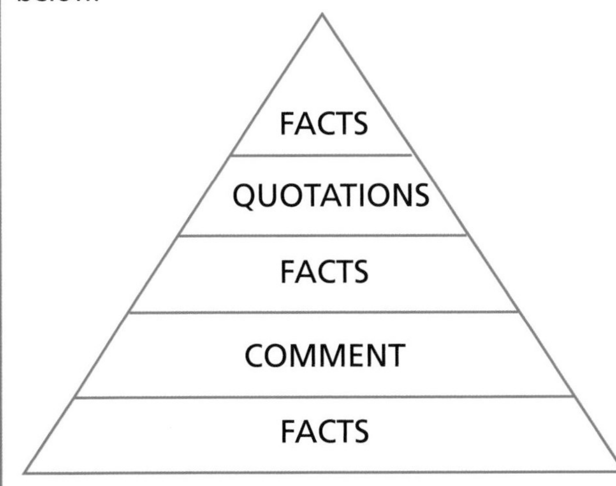

Make sure you include your own opinion of events.

Many Christians today believe it is important to show love to others by serving their community without being paid. They sacrifice both time and money.

TPD
SM
CIT

List all the ways you or others could help others **voluntarily**. It doesn't have to be anything to do with church.

Black Santa

For the last 30 years the Deans from St Ann's Cathedral in Belfast have staged a sit-out in aid of charity, raising thousands of pounds.

The sit-out takes place on the steps of St Ann's Cathedral in the week before Christmas.

At Christmas time many people support campaigns like Operation Christmas Child run since 1990 by 'Samaritan's Purse'.

This campaign asks people to gather up shoe boxes and fill them with small items like toothpaste, toothbrushes, soap, sweets and toys for children who are in need across the world.

The boxes are delivered by volunteers to places like hospitals, refugee shelters, and orphanages.

ICT
BC
TPD
WO

Use a search engine to find the web site of Samaritan's Purse.

In groups, prepare a presentation on Operation Christmas Child. Think about the order of your presentation. If *you* were listening to it, what would you want to know first?

After each group has finished giving their presentation, have a class discussion about it.

Was anything left out? Did it include something you didn't know?

Events leading to the death of Jesus

One way that important stories and teachings are passed on is through festivals.

In this unit you are going to learn about the events that took place in Holy Week, the week leading up to Easter. Easter is one of the most important festivals for Christians.

During Holy Week Christians remember the last week of Jesus' life.

TPD

On your own, write down everything you know about Easter. It doesn't have to be in any order. Just write things down as you think of them. Keep this somewhere safe.

TPD SM

How could you pass on details about your life so that your great, great-grandchildren would know you as well as your friends do now?

What information would you want to pass on?

How would you pass this information on accurately?

MI TPD WO

With a partner, see if you can put the events of Holy Week into the order they happened.

The crucifixion

Jesus' arrest

Jesus carries his cross through Jerusalem.

Jesus before Pilate

The death of Jesus

Jesus is whipped and crowned with thorns.

Jesus is tried by the Jewish court.

Jesus is sentenced by Pilate.

Peter denies Jesus.

Palm Sunday

TPD

Do you know who this is?

Can you think of any other important people or groups who have visited Northern Ireland?

Why did they visit?

Where did they go?

What preparations were made to welcome them?

In springtime at the time of Jesus, hundreds of Jewish families began the journey to Jerusalem, their capital city, to celebrate the festival of Passover.

MI

Look back to pages 31-2 and 60 to read the story of the Passover.

Jesus and his disciples set off for Jerusalem too and were soon joined by other groups of followers on the way.

MI

Read Matthew 21:1-11.

From this passage, how do you know Jesus was popular with ordinary people? Why do you think they waved palm branches?

He was riding a donkey.

Imagine if some of our important visitors to Northern Ireland came in battered old buses!

MI

Are the following statements true or false?

1 Jesus and his disciples were nearly in Jericho
2 He sent four disciples to get a donkey
3 The disciples made a saddle with their coats
4 The crowds cheered Jesus
5 The people threw firs on the road

TPD

Why do you think Jesus rode into Jerusalem on a donkey?

Don't answer this question too quickly! There might be several reasons. Do some research. The Old Testament prophet Zechariah might come into it.

When you have all completed your research, discuss your findings in class.

The Last Supper

Luke 22:7-38

TPD

Have you ever been asked to a special meal to celebrate something important?

Shortly before his death Jesus and his disciples celebrated a Passover meal together.

It was the last meal Jesus would have with his disciples before he died. It had to take place in secret because the religious leaders wanted to kill Jesus.

TPD

Christians today call this meal 'The Last Supper'. Why do you think it is called this?

What two symbols were important in the Last Supper?

What did Jesus say they represented?

Communion

Today, nearly all Christian churches hold special services in obedience to Jesus' command to remember him.

Depending which Christian church a person belongs to, this service can be called **Communion,** the **Breaking of Bread** or the **Eucharist**.

'Eucharist' comes from a Greek word meaning 'Thanksgiving' because Christians thank God for his great love in sending Jesus.

'Communion' means being at one with or in union with someone else and is used by Christians to say that they all belong together because of their beliefs.

The Salvation Army and the Quakers do not hold communion services. They feel that some people might believe they are Christians simply because they take part in Communion.

In some churches the Eucharist is held every day but in others it happens once a week, once a month, or perhaps two or three times a year.

The communion table at St Columba's Parish Church, Omagh

TPD BC

Look at the picture above. Write down as many things as you can that strike you about it.

What do you think it says about the Church of Ireland?

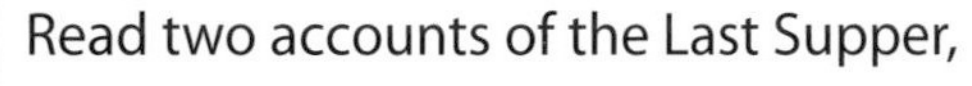

TPD

Read two accounts of the Last Supper,

- Matthew 26:17-30
- Luke 22:7-23

What differences are there between these two accounts?

What similarities are there?

The communion experience in Omagh Community Church

Marianne, a member of Omagh Community Church, describes communion in her church (pictured below).

Communion in our church is about celebrating our relationship with God and thanking him for sending Jesus to die on the cross to enable us to enjoy this relationship with him.

As we are a community church and have people from different backgrounds joining our services, we tend to celebrate communion in varied ways.

Sometimes we hold communion as part of a church meal where we all bring a dish and share fellowship together. We round off the meal as Jesus did by sharing the bread and non-alcoholic wine.

Sometimes during a church service we place a cup and bread at the front of our church beside the cross and during a period of worship families are encouraged to go forward and share in communion.

At other times the cup and bread is passed around the church so that we can encourage each other and share in what symbolises for us Jesus' body and blood.

HOW DO JEWS CELEBRATE PASSOVER TODAY?

TPD BC

Find out what a Passover meal is like in a Jewish family today.

Write an account of a Passover meal.

Judas

The religious leaders had a problem.

They wanted to arrest Jesus and put him to death but they were afraid to do it openly as Jesus was so popular. With perhaps 100,000 Jews in Jerusalem for Passover it was impossible to find and arrest him secretly.

The answer to this problem was Judas Iscariot, one of Jesus' twelve disciples. He went to the religious leaders and offered to **betray** Jesus.

TPD

Why do you think Judas betrayed Jesus?

Here are some possible reasons. Can you think of any more?

Discuss each one and say how likely it is to be true. Do you think one is more likely than others?

1 The devil suggested it to him.

2 He did it for money.

3 He did it for popularity and power.

4 The name 'Iscariot' may mean Zealot and so Judas was disappointed when Jesus did not start a revolt against the Romans.

5 He may have been afraid of what the authorities would do to Jesus and his followers and so he tried to force Jesus into action.

The arrest of Jesus

TPD WO

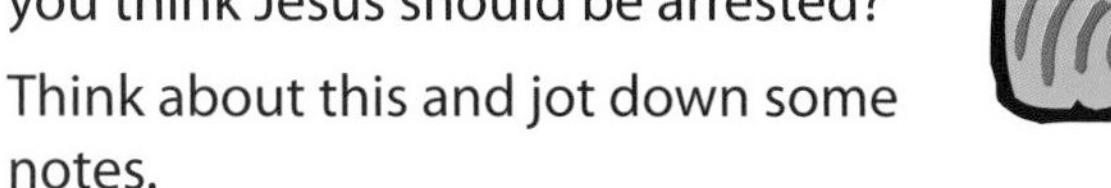

Imagine you are a Pharisee. Why do you think Jesus should be arrested?

Think about this and jot down some notes.

Now organise a class debate on the motion "Jesus is innocent of all charges".

TPD SM PD

It's terrible to be accused of doing something you didn't do.

Has this ever happened to you? If so, do you understand why it happened?

MI

After the Last Supper, Jesus and his disciples went to the Mount of Olives.

Where was this? What did it look like?

Jesus had gone to the Mount of Olives with his disciples to pray. The time was right for Judas to act.

It was night and the place was deserted. Judas slipped away from the others and told the Jewish authorities where Jesus was.

He came back with the Chief Priests, elders and the Temple guards.

Because it was dark it was necessary to give a clear sign to show the guards which one was Jesus. Judas kissed him on the cheek. This was a common greeting and often given from a disciple to a rabbi and was a sign of loyalty, respect and friendship.

However, now it was a sign of betrayal.

TPD

Why did Judas have to show the guards which one was Jesus?

Apart from the fact that it was dark, can you think of any other reasons?

Com
BC
WO

Using mime, and in groups, act out the scene of the arrest of Jesus.

Com
BC
TPD

1 Imagine you are a newspaper reporter present at the arrest of Jesus.

You must have :

- A headline
- A picture
- Interviews

2 Now imagine you are a reporter present when Jesus is arrested. You are reporting live to Sky News as it happens. Give your report.

What is different between the newspaper report and the live report?

For example, have you used different words?

BC
WO

Role-play

It is just after the arrest of Jesus. With a partner, pretend you are two of Jesus' disciples.

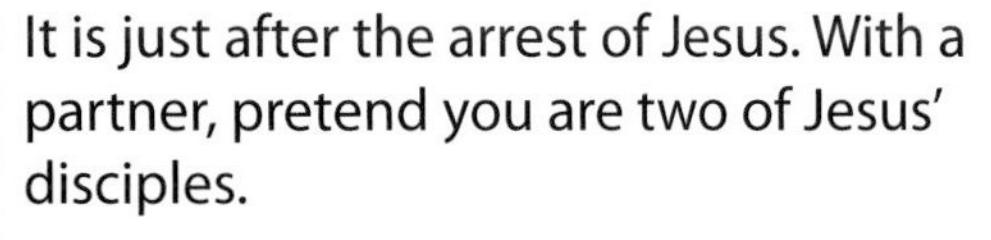

Script a conversation about what has happened and how you feel.

The trials of Jesus

Trial 1: Before the Sanhedrin at night

↓

Trial 2: Before the Sanhedrin at daybreak

↓

Trial 3: Before Pilate

↓

Trial 4: Before Herod

↓

Trial 5: Before Pilate

According to the Gospels Jesus was arrested late on the Thursday night and by the middle of Friday afternoon he was dead.

Because the Jewish Sabbath started on Friday at sunset, no criminal who was Jewish was allowed to remain hanging on a cross.

Between his arrest and crucifixion Jesus was questioned by both the Jewish and Roman authorities.

THE JEWISH TRIAL

Jesus was brought for trial before the **Sanhedrin**. This was the official court of religious leaders which met in the Temple area in Jerusalem to decide matters connected with Jewish law and to deal with any offenders who broke it. The full council was made up of 71 members. You read about this before on page 54.

The chief priests wanted to get Jesus tried, sentenced and put to death quickly. They had to break many legal customs to do so.

Jesus was alone because Peter and the other disciples had deserted him.

TPD
SM

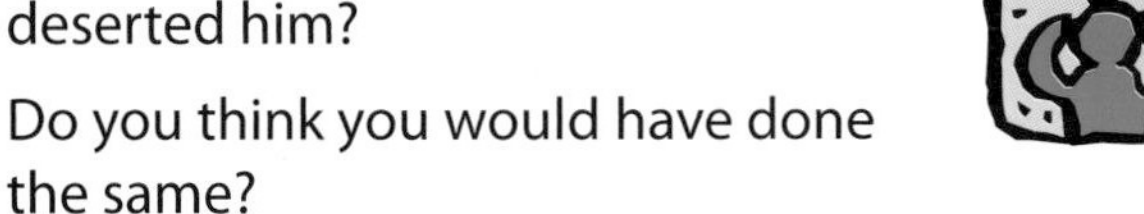

Are you surprised that Jesus' disciples deserted him?

Do you think you would have done the same?

Witnesses were brought in to tell lies about Jesus but they did not agree among themselves. Witnesses who do not tell the truth are often called 'false witnesses'.

Read all about it in Matthew 26:57-67.

Jesus claimed to be the Messiah and that was **blasphemy** for those who did not believe him.

They all agreed Jesus should be put to death, but there was a problem. The Sanhedrin could not condemn anyone to death. Only the Romans could. They needed the support of the Governor. But the Governor was a Roman and would not be interested in a charge of blasphemy.

What could they do?

The charge of blasphemy would simply have to be changed to suit the Romans.

Why was Jesus' trial unfair?

1. The trial took place at night. This was not legal as the Sanhedrin could meet only between sunrise and sunset.
2. The Sanhedrin was not allowed to meet during a festival and this was the time of the Passover Festival.
3. Jesus did not have anyone to defend him.
4. It was unlikely all 71 members of the Sanhedrin were present to give Jesus a fair hearing.

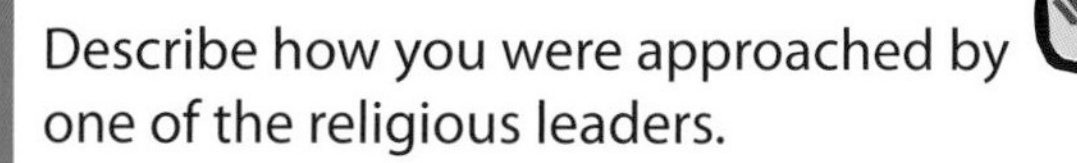

TPD

Imagine you were one of the false witnesses.

Describe how you were approached by one of the religious leaders.

What did they tell you to say and why did you agree to give false evidence?

Peter denies knowing Jesus

TPD PD

Read Matthew 26:69-74.

How would you feel if your best friend pretended that they did not know you?

What would you say to them?

MI BC TPD

Imagine you are Peter.

Write a diary entry for the day you said you didn't know Jesus.

Plan it by imagining how you would have felt and writing down words you might use.

THE ROMAN TRIAL

The Romans recognised the Jewish council as a sort of parliament of the Jews. But they did not allow it to put anybody to death. Only the Roman Governor could pass the death sentence.

Now the chief priests had to persuade Pontius Pilate to confirm and order the execution of Jesus.

Pontius Pilate – who was he?

Judea was a province of the Roman Empire and Pilate was in charge of it.

Judea was a violent and difficult place to govern and Pilate often used his powers to have rebels put to death.

Philo of Alexandria, a Jewish writer, says that Pilate was known for his cruelty and corruption. He hated and despised the Jewish people. He annoyed the Jews by allowing the Roman troops to bring their regimental standards into Jerusalem. The standards had pictures of the Emperor on them, which offended Jewish law.

Another reason for their hatred is that Pilate took Temple money to build an **aqueduct**.

MI
TPD

Find out when Philo of Alexandria lived. Do you think you can trust what he wrote? Why or why not?

Pilate spent most of the year at the Roman Military headquarters at Caesarea. But he came up to Jerusalem at the time of the Jewish festivals in case there was any trouble.

Pilate was married to Claudia. There is a tradition that she became a Christian.

Pilate is best known as the man who put Jesus to death. He believed Jesus was innocent but he didn't want a riot.

He had a choice between setting free Barabbas or Jesus. He agreed to Jesus' death when the crowd shouted for it.

A possible explanation for Pilate's actions is that he wanted to avoid a riot because he didn't want bad reports to get back to his masters in Rome. If that happened, he could be called to appear before the Emperor and answer to him. If the Emperor wasn't pleased with him he might lose his job.

MI
TPD
WO

In groups, carry out some research into Pontius Pilate.

Now your group should think if things that you would like to ask him if you could.

What do you think his answers might be?

Trial before Herod

Luke's gospel tells us of another trial before King Herod who was in Jerusalem at this time.

Pilate sent Jesus to him because he was in control of the area where Jesus had been born. Pilate hoped that Herod would condemn Jesus to save him from having to make a decision.

But Pilate was out of luck!

MI

Say whether these statements are true or false.

1 The Governor usually released one prisoner at the Passover.
2 Barabbas was the High Priest at this time.
3 Pilate offered to release either Jesus or Barabbas.
4 The Jewish leaders told the crowd to ask for the release of Jesus.
5 The crowd cried out for Jesus to be crucified.

Jesus versus Barabbas

These were two very different prisoners. Barabbas was a gang leader who had started riots and committed murder.

Jesus had taught about love and forgiveness and had healed people.

MI

Here are some things that Jesus did say, and didn't say. Decide which are true and which are false.

"This trial is not fair."

"My kingdom is not of this world."

"You are right in saying I am a king."

"I came to bring truth to the world."

"Step outside and we'll sort this out, man to man."

"You would have no power over me if it were not given to you from above."

MI BC TPD WO

Guilty or not guilty?

After only three years' work Jesus was condemned to death for claiming to be the Son of God.

You are going to act out a court scene. The class will be spilt into two. One group is against Jesus being the Son of God and the other group is for Jesus being the Son of God.

You will need to gather evidence.

After gathering the evidence you will need to decide on a prosecutor and a defence lawyer to present the cases.

Here are some suggestions to get you started

He mixes with all the wrong types of people eg tax collectors and lepers.

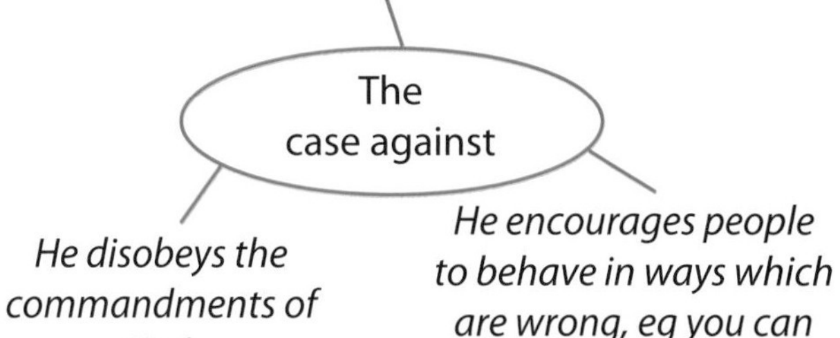

The case for

The road to Calvary and the Crucifixion

TPD PD

What sacrifices do your family and friends make for you?

Would it be a sacrifice if you gave up something you did not really want?

TPD

Read Matthew 27:27-61

How do you think Jesus was feeling at this time?

What about Peter? What about Judas?

In verses 27-31, what do each of the things the soldiers put on Jesus mean?

Crucifixion was a Roman method of execution. It was the penalty for murder, stealing, rebellion and many other offences.

The Romans crucified slaves, foreigners and criminals but not Roman citizens.

After the defeat of the 'rebellion of the slaves' led by the gladiator Spartacus, 6,000 of his followers were crucified along the Appian way between Capua and Rome, in Italy.

Crucifixion was a very long, slow and painful death. Roman soldiers would break the criminal's legs and death by suffocation would soon follow.

Other punishments used by the Romans included being beaten with a whip which was made of strips of leather with pieces of bone attached.

In Jerusalem criminals were usually crucified on a hill called Golgotha, which was just outside the city. Golgotha is a Jewish name which means the 'Place of the Skull'.

The Latin name, Calvary, has the same meaning. No one knows exactly where it was, although it was probably outside one of the gates of Jerusalem by the side of the road.

MI BC

Find out about Spartacus. Write out several paragraphs about him.

Plan your piece of writing beforehand. For example:

How will you begin?

How will you finish?

TPD

The Romans always executed people on a hill.

Why do you think this was?

BC

Imagine that you were a bystander as Jesus carried his cross to Calvary.

Write or draw what you saw as Jesus passed your way.

Simon of Cyrene was an African who had come to Jerusalem to celebrate the Passover. He was watching as Jesus was being led to his death.

Men condemned to crucifixion had to carry their cross. Jesus was so weakened by scourging (whipping) that he was unable to carry his cross.

The Romans made Simon carry it for Jesus.

TPD

Read Matthew 27:51 again.

The curtain separated the Holy of Holies from the rest of the Temple.

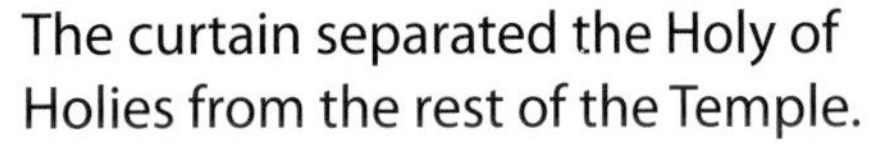

What do you think the significance of this is? Remember what you learnt about the Temple!

In the few centuries after the death of Jesus, many Christians walked in prayerful silence from the Garden of Gethsemane, at the Mount of Olives, to the hill of Calvary, thinking about the suffering and death of Jesus.

During the Crusades, **pilgrims** began to mark certain stopping places on this journey, to recall particular incidents on the Way of the Cross (also called the **Via Dolorosa** meaning 'the way of grief').

St Francis of Assisi and his friars made the tradition of following the **Stations of the Cross** popular.

In many Catholic churches today, there are Stations of the Cross. These are a series of carvings or paintings of the events on the way to the cross and ending with Jesus' burial.

People stop in front of each one, thinking and praying.

MI

BC

How many Stations of the Cross are there?

Name them all.

Now pick two and design your own version of them.

Don't just copy from real ones – make up your own!

MI

BC

Do some research on the Roman army. How was it made up?

Who was in charge of each part of it?

Make a classroom display about it.

Include a sign which says at the top: "We found our information from. . ." and then list your sources.

TPD

WO

'Cent' means 100.

Divide into groups.

See how many words containing 'cent' you can think of. The group with the most is the winner.

A company of soldiers was always on duty to guard prisoners who were to be crucified to see that the crucifixion was properly carried out and to prevent any rescue bid.

BC

Use the following words to make up 15 sentences about the death of Christ:

Gethsemane	High Priest
Judas	trial
Pilate	crucified
robe	darkness
robbers	Calvary
soldiers	mocked
Temple	finished
died	

New York Christians participate in 'The Way of the Cross' walk on Good Friday.

GOOD FRIDAY

Good Friday is the day set aside by Christians to remember Jesus' death. It is the most solemn day in the church calendar and in the past was known as 'Black Friday'.

Churches often remove flowers and other items of decoration from display or cover them up because it is seen as a day of mourning.

TPD

Many Christians go to church on Good Friday. Churches often hold services between 12 noon and 3.00 pm.

Why do you think this is?

In some towns, Christians of different denominations gather together to walk behind someone carrying a cross through the streets and then to a church service.

In Spain and some other countries, people who are very sorry for the things they have done wrong (called 'Penitents') walk through the streets wearing long robes with hoods and carrying a big cross of wood.

Some Christians **fast** on Good Friday. This helps them remember the sacrifice Jesus made for them on the day of the crucifixion. Others might avoid certain foods like meat and eat fish instead.

It is traditional to eat hot cross buns on Good Friday. The pastry cross on top of the buns and reminds Christians of the cross that Jesus died on.

TPD

Why is Good Friday called this? It might not be simple – you'll have to do a bit of research.

ICT
MI
BC

Like so many people today, Jesus was mocked and killed for his faith.

Find out about people who have had to die for their faith in the past or who are suffering for their faith at the present time.

Present your findings in a Word document.

MI
Cit

People are not persecuted just for their religious beliefs.

Find out about Nelson Mandela who was imprisoned in South Africa for his beliefs between 1963 and 1990.

You could present your findings to the class.

CAPITAL PUNISHMENT

Capital punishment, also called the death penalty, is the execution of a convicted criminal by the state.

Crucifixion was one of the most common forms of capital punishment and it was still being used up until the nineteenth century in Japan.

In 1969 capital punishment became illegal in Great Britain, followed by Northern Ireland in 1973.

From 1957 only hanging was allowed as the form of capital punishment. Capital punishment is still legal in Jersey for murder, but no one has been executed there since 1959.

In some parts of the world, such as the USA, capital punishment is still used. The most common form is death by **lethal** injection.

TPD
Cit
PD

Take some time to think about the arguments for and against capital punishment. You could make two lists on a piece of paper.

Which arguments seem to you to be stronger?

Now organise a class debate on the motion "This house believes that capital punishment should be re-introduced in this country".

TPD

Why do Christians believe Jesus had to die?

Choose the correct statements from the list:

1 To prove he was the Son of God

2 To make himself a hero

3 To return to heaven

4 Because he knew he had to pay the price for mankind's sins

Above Jesus' cross there was a notice written in three languages.

The Latin inscription was ***Iesvs Nazarenvs Rex Ivdaeorvm*** meaning 'Jesus of Nazareth, King of the Jews'. This was the crime that Jesus was accused of.

This inscription is often attached to crucifixes, above Jesus' head, in its shortened form ***INRI***.

iStockphoto/Holger Franke

MI

Make a list of all the supernatural events that occurred at the time of Jesus' death.

Timetable of the crucifixion

9.00 am – Jesus was placed on the cross.

12.00 noon – Darkness came over the land.

Just before his death some of the gospels record words spoken by Jesus.

In Luke, Jesus speaks to one of the thieves on a cross beside him.

In John, he speaks to his mother.

Mark records the final words of Jesus, spoken in **Aramaic**. (Mark15:34)

3.00 pm – Jesus died.

SM WO PD

In groups talk about a time when you felt lonely and deserted.

How did the situation arise? What did it feel like?

How did it end up?

As he was dying, Jesus called in his own language:-

Eloi,
Eloi, lama
sabachthani?

MI TPD

Find out what this means in Matthew 27:46. Write down the meaning.

Why do you think Jesus said this?

Com TPD BC

Imagine you were a member of the execution squad which crucified Jesus.

Write a letter to a friend in Rome describing what happened.

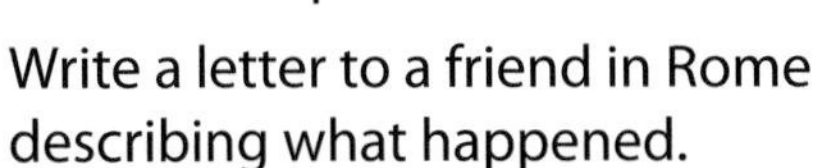

Remember this is a letter to a friend. Use appropriate language.

Com ICT MI BC

Imagine you are one of the following: a Roman official; a soldier; a reporter.

You have to compile a report about the crucifixion of Jesus.

In your report you need to include:

a. A factual account of the crucifixion

b. Interviews with:
   - Simon of Cyrene
   - One of the women bystanders
   - The officer on duty at the cross
   - A Temple official

Remember this is an official report. Use the right language.

JESUS' DEATH

Read the football sketch below.

Two children are passing a football to each other.

Boy: Let's see what damage I can do to that window!

Other boy: Don't be stupid!

Boy: What's the matter with you! You're not 'chicken' are you?

Other boy: [Looks away]

Boy: (Takes a massive kick at the ball and it breaks a neighbour's window.)

Neighbour: [angry] Oi! That's my window you've broken!

Boy: [Hangs his head]

Neighbour: That's a *lot* of money that is. It's not ordinary glass you know! It will cost a fortune to repair that, and I want *you* to pay for it.

Boy: [Looks worried] How am I going to pay for it?

Neighbour: That's *not* my problem! I want this repaired *now*!

Boy: But I can't!

Parent: [Walks onto the scene] I see that there is a problem here.

Neighbour: Yes, there certainly is a problem! My window has been broken by this child, and I want it paid for now!

Parent: [Puts his hand into his pocket and pulls out a bundle of money] Here, this should cover all your expenses and pay for all the trouble this has caused you.

Neighbour: Thanks, that should more than cover it. No hard feelings then?

Boy and Parent: No. Bye!

Can you see any similarities between this story and the life and death of Jesus?

Afterwards ...

After Jesus died the disciples were alone and afraid. They did not know what to do next.

One disciple in particular felt really bad ...

Judas was ashamed of his behaviour. In order to try to ease his guilty conscience he returned to the High Priest the money he had been given for betraying Jesus.

They refused the money, saying it was blood money. Judas left the money with them even so and it was later used to buy a field to bury strangers in. This field has been called the Field of Blood.

So what happened to Judas?

Sadly, Judas ended his own life.

BC
TPD
PD

Imagine that by means of time travel you have been able to arrange an interview with Judas just before he died.

What questions would you like to ask him?

What answers do you think he might give?

What do *you* think of what Judas did?

The new covenant or agreement between God and man

The Old Covenant

In Old Testament days, people had to offer sacrifices to God in order to have their sins forgiven.

The person had to put their hands on the animal and this signalled that they were identifying themselves with it.

When they killed the animal the person was acknowledging that they deserved to die because of their sins but that the animal was taking their place.

The animal had to be young and healthy. This was to prove how much the person loved God. They believed that God would not accept an imperfect animal.

This wasn't a **permanent** solution to sin so the act had to be repeated. In Jesus' day the sacrifices were carried out by the High Priest in the Temple.

The New Covenant

Whenever Jesus died, the curtain separating the main part of the Temple from the Holy of Holies tore in two.

Christians believe that this meant that the people no longer had to go through the High Priest in order to get close to God. They can come to him though Jesus.

Through the New Covenant, Christians believe that those who are sorry and accept Jesus as their saviour, are forgiven.

Animal sacrifices are no longer needed as Jesus was the sacrifice.

Resurrection and Ascension of Jesus

The meaning of Easter

Jesus' death is not the end of his story.

In this unit you will learn that Christians believe that after Jesus' death he came back to life and visited his friends and followers once more and that he then went to heaven to be with God, his Father.

Easter Sunday (or Easter Day) is the oldest and most important Christian festival.

It is when Christians celebrate how, three days after being killed, Jesus rose from the dead. This event is called the **Resurrection**.

Sunday is the day when most Christian services are held.

TPD

Why do you think the Christian holy day is Sunday?

WHEN IS EASTER?

Easter usually comes in the month of April.

It is called a 'moveable' feast because the date is fixed according to the moon.

Easter Sunday is the first Sunday after the full moon that occurs after the spring **equinox** on 21st March.

MI
TPD
WO

What things do you associate with Easter?

Brainstorm your ideas.

Now divide into groups. Each group should take one thing, eg Easter eggs, and find out why they are associated with Easter. Find out as much as you can.

Below, find out how James, a 13 year old Northern Irish boy, celebrates Easter.

"Often my family attends a Sunrise service which is held on a hilltop at 6.00 am.

Services like these are held on hilltops all over Northern Ireland.

I attend a service at Knockmany which is near Augher, Co Tyrone.

When we get home we have boiled egg for breakfast. Then we go to church.

For lunch we have roast lamb with mint sauce and vegetables. Then we would have some simnel cake.

I look forward most of all to eating my chocolate Easter Egg, especially the sweets inside."

TPD

What is simnel cake? What is symbolic about it?

BC

Design a symbol that shows something of the meaning that Easter has for Christians.

Com TPD Cit

Easter eggs go on sale the day after Boxing Day.

Look up a dictionary to find the meaning of the word 'commercialise'.

Now have a class debate on the motion:

"This house believes Easter has become too commercialised."

The women at the tomb

TPD

What does 'anoint' mean?

Why was this done to someone after they died?

There had been no time to anoint the body of Jesus. Instead it had been taken down from the cross, wrapped in linen and laid in the tomb. A heavy stone sealed the entrance.

TPD

Why had there been no time to anoint Jesus' body?

Traditionally it was the responsibility of women to anoint bodies with spices and ointments. Three of the women who were followers of Jesus were at the tomb early on the Sunday morning.

We do not know much about the women. Mary Magdalene means Mary from the city of Magdala which was three miles from Capernaum. Possibly all three women were from Galilee and had helped Jesus with his work there.

The women were amazed to find the tomb unguarded and the stone which had been used to seal the entrance had been rolled away.

What had happened?

Read all about what happened in Matthew 28:1-10.

iStockphoto/Tim Kimberley

The tomb where Jesus' body was put probably looked something like this.

MI

Write a summary of this account using the five 'Ws':

Who?

Where?

What?

When?

Why?

MI TPD

Now read Luke's account of what happened in Luke 24:1-12.

What is the same in these two accounts?

What is different?

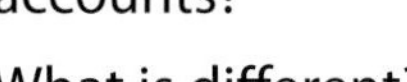

Can you find another account of this in another gospel?

Pick people to read the parts in this play. Now perform it in class.

Easter Morning

Characters: Thomas, John, Peter, eight other disciples and Mary

Thomas: Quiet!

Two: Why? What?

Three: Sshh!

John: Did you hear something?

Thomas: Quiet! I think, *(pause)* maybe, maybe I did.

Five: Look, we can't just stay here!

Two: I've got to get out of here!

Thomas: Quiet, you'll give us all away.

Three: He's right, you know. Leave now and they'll catch you and it will be the death of us all.

John: Let's stay calm. We hide here till things blow over, and then we can slip away at night, maybe in a couple of days or so. *(Five walks over to Two)*

Thomas: And if they catch any of us, what then?

Three: Well, it's our word against theirs. We should just deny that we ever *(his words trail off)* knew him. *(Those who are talking, look over at Peter who sits despondent and alone)*

John: Well, what would you have done? Would you have said you didn't know him, like Peter did?

Thomas: No! ... Well ...

Two: I, I can't say, maybe.

John: I thought no, certainly not, but I'm so confused. It seems hopeless. Why didn't he save himself?

Five: This isn't really happening. Jesus wouldn't have abandoned us. I know, I'm going to wake up soon. I know it. *(starts talking louder)* It's like when you're falling, I know *(almost shouting now)* I know I'm going to wake up soon!

Thomas: Sshh!

Five: You Sshh! I'm going to wake up! This nightmare will be over.

(There is a pause in the dialogue, all is quiet; then ...)

Peter: I denied him but I didn't kill him. I tried to save him. It was I who drew my sword, only I. I tried to defend him but he wouldn't let me.

Two: Let's go.

Peter: Yes, let's go. If they capture us, they'll kill us. It's just as well.

Two: Are you crazy? I want to go. I want to escape, I want to live.

Thomas: They'll catch us and we'll surely die.

John: *(To Peter)* What, what are you talking about?

Peter: It's Mary, She's coming, John.

John: Quickly! Come in.

Mary: John, Peter. He's gone! He's not there, he's gone!

Peter: Calm down. Mary, what are you saying?

Mary: Calm down? How can you ask me to calm down when the body of Jesus is no longer in the tomb?

John: What!?

Mary: We went to the tomb with the myrrh and frankincense to anoint his body and he was gone!

Peter: No! It can't be.

Mary: He's gone! *(Peter pushes past and runs away)*

John: Peter! *(John runs after them, the other nine start to mumble and talk loudly to each other about what has just happened)*

Thomas: He can't be gone. There were Temple guards at the tomb entrance.

Mary: I tell you, Thomas, he's gone!

Thomas: You must have been at the wrong tomb.

Mary: No! We knew which tomb it was. It was sealed with a large boulder and we were wondering if we'd have to bribe the Temple guards to open it for us, but when we got there, the stone was completely rolled away and the tomb was empty.

Thomas: But the guards at the entrance! How could he be gone?

Mary: He's gone, we were at the *right* tomb!

Five: The stone?

Mary: I don't know how the stone moved and I don't care. What matters is that we were looking for someone who was alive, amongst the dead.

Thomas: What nonsense.

Mary: Wait; you have to hear all my story. I know I'm babbling but it's just too much. We were standing there crying. The stone was moved, his body gone. We didn't know what to do. Then suddenly two men in shinning clothing were standing there, we were so scared we fell to the ground. I dropped the oil and it smashed. I was trembling. But they said "Why do you look for the living among the dead? He is not here, he has risen!"

Thomas: Dreamers! We saw him die! Crucified, nailed to a cross. Jesus is dead.

Mary: Yes, he died, but he has risen.

Thomas: Impossible, it's over. It's time to go home. Give him up, Mary.

Mary: It's not over, it's just beginning.

Two: Peter's coming back! *(Peter and John run back)*

Five: Peter, what did you see?

Peter: Mary was right, I went into the tomb before John and there were strips of linen but that's all.

Five: What can it mean?

Peter: I don't know.

John: What can it mean?

Mary: *(excited)* John, you know!

John: What can it mean? Don't you see? He's alive! He has risen from the dead!

Peter: Can it be?

John: It has to be. He is alive! Let's be happy!

TPD
BC

Can you imagine how Mary felt?

Draw faces with the expression on Mary's face to show how she must have felt at each of these times:

At the Crucifixion

On the way to the tomb

Meeting the angels

Meeting Jesus

Telling the disciples

TPD
SM
PD

Imagine a line right along the floor of your classroom.

Someone reads this statement: "The women who followed Jesus were more faithful than the men."

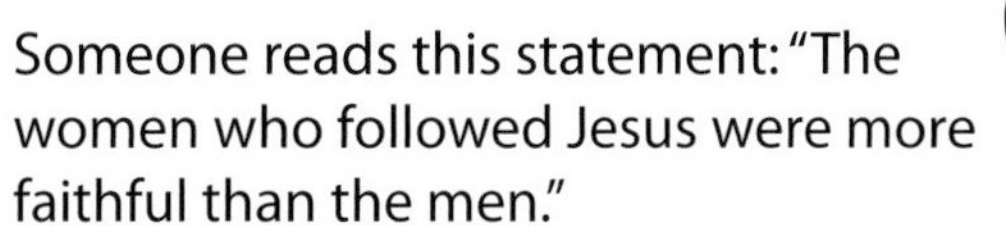

One end of the line is for people who completely agree with the statement. The other end is for people who completely disagree. But you might be somewhere in between!

Stand on the line between the two viewpoints according to your opinion. Remember you need to be able to say why you take this position on the line.

MI
TPD
WO
PD

Some people have tried to argue that Jesus did not rise from the dead. You can read what they say below.

1 Jesus' body could have been stolen and the disciples pretended or thought he'd risen.

2 Some say that the disciples only *thought* they saw Jesus after he had risen.

3 Some say Jesus never died on the cross but fainted and came round again.

4 Some say Jesus never really rose from the dead but is only alive through his teaching.

Form into four groups and each group discuss one of these.

Now think about all you have read and learned. What do you think of these statements?

TPD
WO

Think about these questions and have a class discussion.

1 Did Jesus really die on the cross? Who thought so? (Mark 15:44)

2 Even if Jesus had recovered, what sort of condition would he have been in? (John 19:1-24)

3 What obstacles were there for such a weak man if he were to escape? (Matthew 27:59-60)

4 Jesus appeared many times to the disciples afterwards. Can any of the details about these appearances not be explained if Jesus was still an ordinary, very weak, human being? (Luke 24:31-36; John 20:19)

Why is the Resurrection important to Christians?

1 The Resurrection proves to Christians that Jesus is alive today in the world through the Holy Spirit. This gives them confidence and encouragement.

2 Christianity is centred on the belief that Jesus is the Son of God, the Messiah, and the Resurrection helps to prove this.

3 Jesus defeated death, giving Christians confidence that through their faith they too can have eternal life.

TPD
SM
WO
PD

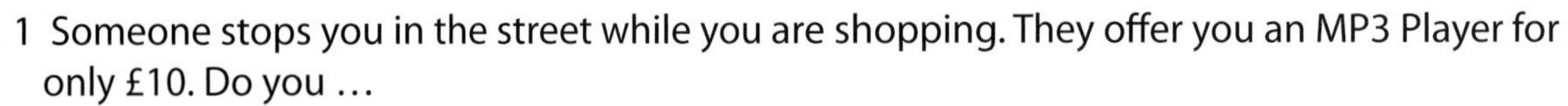

Do you believe everything people say? Test yourself!

1 Someone stops you in the street while you are shopping. They offer you an MP3 Player for only £10. Do you …
(a) refuse to buy it?
(b) ask them for the guarantee?
(c) buy it?

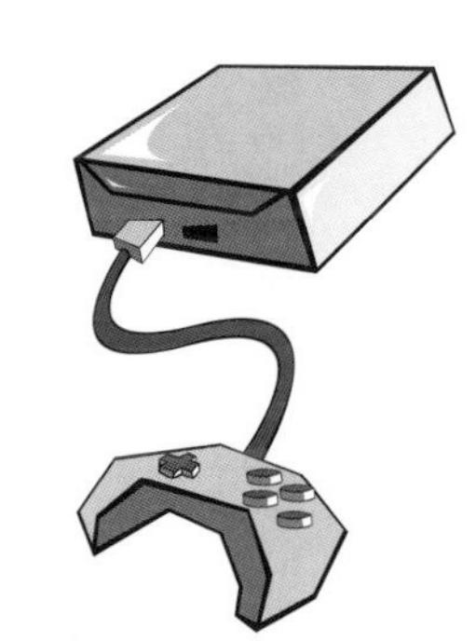

2 If a friend tells you that they receive £60 a week pocket money, do you ...
(a) laugh?
(b) ask to see the money?
(c) immediately demand more money from *your* parents or carers?

3 A friend borrows your favourite Xbox game for a few days. A month later do you ...
(a) ask for it back?
(b) drop a hint ?
(c) forget about it?

4 When practical jokes are played, are you ...
(a) always the one to spot any trick?
(b) usually the one to spot the joke coming but occasionally fall for it?
(c) always the one to fall for it?

5 When playing sport would you describe yourself as ...
(a) very competitive?
(b) quite competitive?
(c) easy-going?

6 UTV Live at Six news programme reveals that aliens have landed in Northern Ireland. What do you do?
(a) Switch off?
(b) Listen to it and text your friends about it?
(c) Spread rumours that you are living next door to an alien?

Count up the number of As, Bs and Cs. Look up your score:

Mostly As: You are quite cynical.
Mostly Bs: You are prepared to think things through.
Mostly Cs: You have faith in people.

In groups, discuss which of these is the best sort of character to have – A, B, or C.

Remember there isn't always a clear answer to a question!

MI
BC
TPD

What is an epitaph?

This is the epitaph on the gravestone of poet WB Yeats, Drumcliffe church, Sligo.

Draw the outline of a tombstone and write an epitaph for Jesus. What could you say about him?

TPD PD

Is there life after this life?

This is an important question. Have you ever wondered about it?

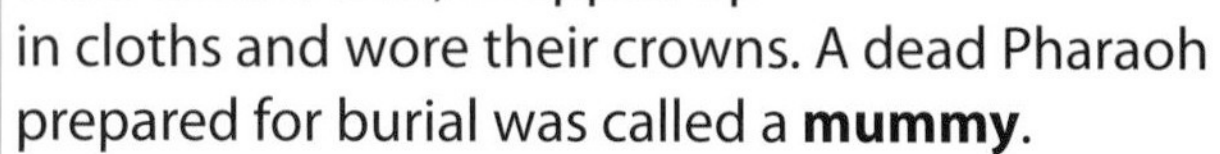

Resurrection is not a new idea!

The Pharaohs of Egypt

When the Pharaohs died they were **embalmed**, wrapped up in cloths and wore their crowns. A dead Pharaoh prepared for burial was called a **mummy**.

The pyramids of Egypt are very famous. They were tombs for Pharaohs. Inside a pyramid was a maze of secret passages which led to the burial chamber where the Pharaoh was laid. When they were buried in them, food, clothing, treasures and money were also put in the tomb.

The Pharaohs believed that they would need these things in the next life. The Egyptians did not believe that death was the end.

The Vikings

The old warriors of Scandinavia were called Vikings. They sailed the seas in long boats raiding many countries including Ireland.

When a Viking king died he was prepared for the next life. His body was placed in a Viking ship and it was loaded with food, money, weapons, slaves and horses. The ship was then set adrift far out in the ocean.

The King was ready and was on his way to another life. They said it was a place called Valhalla, where brave warriors rested.

Christians believe in life after death because of what happened with Jesus. At the end of time they believe that Jesus will return to judge. Those who have lived the way Jesus wanted them to, will join God and those who have not will be separated from God.

This explains what Christians mean when they talk of heaven and hell.

TPD

What images come to your mind when you think of heaven and hell?

Write them down. What evidence is there for the things you have written down?

Other religions, such as Hinduism, believe that when someone dies his soul moves into a new body to live another life.

This is known as **reincarnation.**

There are some people who say that this life is the only one. There is no afterlife.

But how are Christians sure that Jesus rose from the dead?

Over 500 people saw Jesus alive.

MI TPD

Each of these references mentions an eyewitness. Look them up and write out their names. Set out your findings in a table like this.

Bible reference	Eyewitnesses
John 20:18 John 21:1 Luke 24:13-16 John 20:26-28 1 Corinthians 15:3-8	

BC

Draw a cross into your notebook and copy the following verse into it:

John 11:25

Com
BC
TPD

Imagine you are a TV producer. You are making a programme about the Resurrection. What music would you choose as background for the following scenes?

1 The women setting off for the tomb
2 The women find the stone has been rolled away and the tomb is empty
3 After the women have spoken to the angel

Bribes! Lies! Corruption!

In Matthew 28:11-15 we learn that the Chief Priests and elders bribed the soldiers with a large sum of money to say that the disciples had come during the night and stolen the body of Jesus.

TPD

Why do you think the Chief Priests bribed the soldiers?

Com
TPD

Imagine you are the soldiers guarding the tomb.

Choose one person to try to persuade the other men in your company to accept this bribe.

Peter and John at the tomb

John 20:1-9

Sometimes when we are told things, we need to check the facts and that's exactly what Peter and one of the other disciples did when they found out the tomb was empty.

MI

Look up the verse references from John 20 and write out the following, filling in the missing words.

Verse 1: ____________________ went to Simon Peter and John and told them what had happened.

Verses 6 and 7: Simon Peter went to the tomb and saw ____________________.

Verse 8: ____________ went into the tomb and he ____________________.

The Emmaus Road

Luke 24:13-35

It is always difficult when you lose a close friend. Perhaps you fall out or maybe one of you has to move house or school.

Jesus' disciples and followers had lost a close friend when he died *but* they did not realise that they were going to see him again.

In this story Jesus appeared to two of his followers. That changed everything for them. They went from being depressed to feeling really happy.

MI TPD

Copy out the sentences below choosing the correct answers from the words in brackets.

1 Two disciples were walking to (Coleraine, Armagh, Emmaus).

2 A man joined them but they did not (say hello, recognise him, see him).

3 It was (Jesus, Herod, Judas).

4 Jesus asked why they were so (happy, sad, glad).

5 They told him (Peter, John, Jesus) had been killed.

6 They also told him that some women said Jesus had (walked, risen, slept) but they did not believe them.

7 Jesus said 'You are slow to (run, think, understand)'.

8 The men invited Jesus for a (meal, party, show).

9 When Jesus gave (thanks, money) for his food they recognised him.

10 Jesus then (disappeared, evaporated, jumped) out of their sight.

TPD

What do you think of the accounts of the appearance of Jesus to the woman at the tomb and Jesus on the Emmaus Road?

Does anything puzzle you about them?

Com BC

Imagine you were one of the disciples on the road to Emmaus.

Write a letter to a friend describing the incident and the effect it had on you.

Commissioning of the eleven

Before Jesus returned to heaven he gave his disciples some very clear information about how to carry on his work. He gave them a **commission**.

Read about what happened in Matthew 28:16-20.

TPD SM PD

Have you ever been picked for a sports team?

How would you feel if you were selected to play for your county or country?

Would you expect the team captain to give you instructions that would help you win the game?

MI TPD

1 What four instructions were the disciples given before Jesus' ascension?

2 What is meant by the word evangelism?

3 Can you give an example of a modern day evangelist?

4 What different types of mission are Christians involved in?

MI TPD Cit

Do you know what 'the third world' is? If not, find out.

Now discuss this statement:

"We need missionaries in our country today, just as much as they are needed in the third world."

Rebekah Bleakley, an 'A' Level Student from Clogher, Co Tyrone describes how she believes she carried out Jesus' command in Matthew 28:16-20.

"During the summer of 2006, I went to Kenya, East Africa, on a project organised by my church.

One of our main purposes was to paint the large Christian Academy in Kapenguria, run under the joint leadership and work of four missionaries.

Our other aim was to evangelise, to reach out to the lost in the surrounding areas and communities.

It was the experience of a lifetime. Not only did we get a taste of Kenyan culture – the food, the dress, the economy, the wildlife, but we also saw the negative side to the nation. Little children suffering from sever hunger or malaria with no hope of help or medicine – likely to die. Adults, some drunk on their own brew, living in what we would call shanty towns, the elderly living under the effects of poverty.

It truly opened the eyes of myself and my friends that indeed there is work to do for God in Africa but we were reminded that there is also great work to do in India, Russia, Spain, England, Northern Ireland – in fact in 'all the world'."

The Ascension

Acts 1:6-11

TPD SM PD

How would you feel if one of your friends came into school one day and announced that they were **emigrating** to Canada?

How would you feel?

What would you do?

How could you keep in contact with them?

Jesus' disciples were facing something like this.

They were about to lose their best friend. He was going to disappear into the sky in front of their very eyes!

To ascend means to go up and on Ascension Day, which is celebrated on the Thursday which falls 40 days after Easter, Christians remember how Jesus left his disciples.

Jesus had spent these 40 days with his disciples instructing them about how to carry on his work after he left.

In some churches special services are held on Ascension Day. In the Church of Ireland diocese of Clogher, an adult Confirmation Service is traditionally held in St Macartin's Cathedral on Ascension Thursday.

TPD

Look at the smallest circle.

Where did Jesus want them to begin their witnessing? Why?

Next look at the second circle. Where were they to go to next? Who lived here?

Now look at the largest circle. Who lived here?

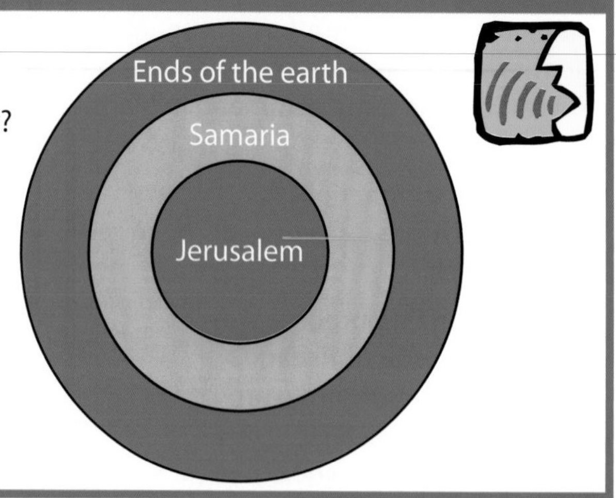

MI

1 What instructions did Jesus give his disciples?
2 Jesus promised his disciples a special helper. Who was it?
3 Who appeared to give the followers a special message?
4 What event were the angels referring to?
5 List the names of the disciples. (Remember there are only eleven now. Why is this?)

Com MI BC

Jerusalem TV is preparing Prime Time reports on rumours about the ascension of Jesus.

As a reporter you have to:

1 Give a brief introduction about the death and reported resurrection of Jesus.
2 Interview one of the apostles about the rumours of Jesus' ascension.

Sample questions:

What is your name?

How did you know Jesus of Nazareth?

What effect did his death have on you?

What did you hear, see, feel on this occasion?

Who else witnessed this event?

What meaning does this event have for you?

What effect has it had on you and the others who witnessed it?

The coming of the Holy Spirit

The Jewish festival of Pentecost, celebrating the giving of the Law to Moses, would have taken place 50 days after the Passover.

This is because Jews believe that it was fifty days after leaving Egypt – after the Passover – that Moses received the Ten Commandments on Mount Sinai.

So between the Ascension and Pentecost Jesus' disciples would have had to spend days without a concrete plan of action, waiting, wondering what to do next.

TPD SM

When have you found it difficult to wait for something?

What would you have felt after the Ascension if you were one of the disciples?

What would you do?

SM WO PD

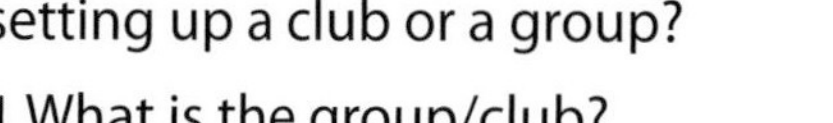

Have any of you ever been involved in setting up a club or a group?

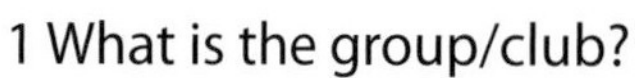

1 What is the group/club?

2 Who was involved in setting it up?

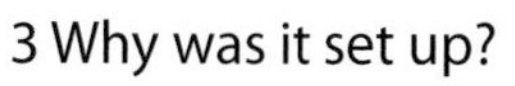

3 Why was it set up?

4 Why did other people get interested in the group?

Glossary

Please note that the definitions given below relate to the work covered in this textbook. Some words may also have alternative meanings, eg 'contract'.

AD: Short for *Anno Domini* which is Latin for 'Year of Our Lord'. AD with a date shows that the date is after the birth of Christ.

Apartheid: Keeping people of different colours apart in society

Apocrypha: Books that are included in some Bibles between the Old and New Testaments. Also called the Deuterocanonical books.

Aqueduct: A man-made channel built to carry water from one place to another.

Aramaic: The language spoken by Jesus. It is still spoken today in parts of Syria and Lebanon.

Aristocratic: To do with the rich and important people in the country

Asphyxiation: A cause of death by not being able to breath properly

Bar Mitzvah: The coming of age ceremony for a Jewish boy

Bat Mitzvah: The coming of age ceremony for a Jewish girl

BC: Short for 'Before Christ'. BC after a date shows that the date is before the birth of Christ.

Benign: Not dangerous. Often used to describe tumours which are not cancerous.

Betray: To be disloyal to your friend or your country, when people thought they could trust you

Betrothed: Like being engaged to be married, but even more serious. It was hard to break a betrothal.

Birthright: The right of a child to inherit possessions and money from his father

Canaan: The land promised by God to the Israelites in the Old Testament. Later it was called Palestine and Israel.

Capital punishment: Putting someone to death for a really serious crime

Centurion: An officer in the Roman army

Codex: A really early form of book, with pages instead of being rolled up as a scroll

Commission: A duty or task given to a person or group to carry out

Communion: The taking of bread and wine as part of a Christian service to remember the Last Supper that Jesus had with his disciples. Also called the Eucharist.

Contract: A agreement made between two people or organisations

Corinth: A port in southern Greece. In ancient times, Corinth was very large and rich.

Corinthians: People who live in Corinth

Corrupt: Spoiled; not good any more

Covenant: A binding agreement

Crucifixion: A way of putting someone to death by nailing or tying a person to a wooden cross by their hands and feet

Day of Atonement: Also called 'Yom Kippur'. A Jewish holiday where Jews fast and prayers are said in the Synagogue.

Dead Sea Scrolls: Scrolls that were found in stone jars hidden in caves along the shores of the Dead Sea. Some of the scrolls contain very early copies of parts of the Old Testament.

Deuterocanonical: Books that are included in some Bibles between the Old and New Testaments. Also called the Apocrypha.

Disciple: A learner or a follower of a religious teacher

Dowry: The money or property a girl's family gave to her husband's family when they got married

Eclipse: When the shadow of one planet falls on the surface of another one, making it look dark. For example, when the Earth is between the sun and the moon, the shadow of the Earth falls on the surface of the moon.

Embalm: To rub oil and spices onto a dead body

Emigrate: To leave your own country to live in another one. No-one makes you do it; you do it because you want to.

Epitaph: Something written in memory of someone who has died. Often put on their gravestone.

Equinox: When day and night are of the same length. It happens twice every year.

Eucharist: The taking of bread and wine as part of a Christian service to remember the Last Supper that Jesus had with his disciples

Exclude: leave out, or keep out, someone or something

Execute: To kill someone after they have been found guilty of a very serious crime

Exile: Being made to live far away from your own country against your will

Exodus: When the Israelites left Egypt, led by Moses

Faith: Being sure of the truth of some religious beliefs

Fast: To eat nothing for a much longer time than usual

Forefather: A member of your family who lived long ago, long before you were born

Garrotte: To kill someone by strangling them

Gentile: A person who is not a Jew

Gethsemane: The garden in Jerusalem where Jesus was betrayed by Judas

Glean: To pick up left-over grain from the fields after they have been harvested

Hanukkah: Jewish festival of lights commemorating the re-dedication of the Temple by Judas Maccabaeus in 165BC (also spelt Hanukah or Chanukah)

Haran: An ancient city. It was in what is now south-east Turkey.

Hereditary: Being handed down through the same family. For example, land passing down from father to son.

Holy of Holies: The innermost room in the Temple of Jerusalem. Only the High Priest was allowed to go into it.

Hypocrite: A person who pretends to believe something when he doesn't really believe it

Idol: Something, such as a statue, that is worshipped as a god

Idolatry: The worship of idols

Inferior: Not as good as something else

Kippah: The skullcap worn by Jewish men, specially when they are praying

Kosher: Food prepared according to the Jewish food laws

Legion: A unit in the Roman army made up of between three to six thousand men

Leper: A person suffering from the disease called leprosy

Leprosy: A disease which makes the sufferer lose feeling in parts of the body. This means that they can injure themselves because they do not feel when they are hurt.

Lesions: Marks or changes in parts of the body (usually inside) which show that there may be something going wrong

Lethal: Deadly

Martyr: Someone who dies for what they believe in

Massoretes: The school of Rabbis that produced the *Mesora*, the text of the Hebrew Bible. They worked on it between the 6th and the 10th centuries AD.

Menorah: A seven-branched candlestick

Midian: The name of one of the sons of Abraham. His descendants, the Midianites, are mentioned often in the Old Testament.

Militant: Feeling so strongly about something that you *do* something about it – you don't just talk about it

Monotheistic: The belief there is only one God

Mount Sinai: The mountain where Moses is said to have received the Ten Commandments from God. It was somewhere on the Arabian peninsula but we are not sure if it was the same mountain that is called that today.

Nomadic: People who move from place to place in search of food and pasture

NSPCC: National Society for the Prevention of Cruelty to Children

Papyrus: Paper made from the stems of the papyrus reed

Parable: A short story that uses familiar things to make a religious or moral point

Parchment: The skin of certain animals, such as sheep, which has been treated to make it easy to write on

Passover: A Jewish festival in memory of when God killed the firstborn of the Egyptians, but spared ('passed over') the Jews

Pentecost: When Christians remember the Holy Spirit coming to the disciples. Often thought of a the birthday of the Church.

Perk: Something good that you might get as a result of doing something else. For example, getting free travel if you work for a travel company.

Permanent: Fixed; something that will stay

Pharaoh: The ruler or king of Egypt

Pilgrim: Someone who goes on a journey to a holy place

Plague: A very bad disease causing the death of a lot of people

Polytheistic: The belief that there is more than one god

Prefect: A senior Roman commander or governor

Prefix: A word which is attached to the beginning of another word to make a new word (eg, in the word monoplane, 'mono' is a prefix)

Prejudice: A dislike of something or a particular group of people for no good reason

Prodigal: spending a lot of money in silly ways

Rabbi: A Jewish religious teacher

Resurrection: The rising of Jesus from the dead three days after his crucifixion

Repentance: Being really sorry for having done wrong

Sabbath: This is the name given by Jews to the seventh day of the week, their holy day. It begins at sunset on Friday and continues to sunset on Saturday.

Sanhedrin: The top legal, religious, and administrative council of the Jews, made up of 71 members, in New Testament times

Samaritans: People who lived in Samaria. The Jews didn't like the Samaritans.

Scribe: The people in Jesus' time who could write and so they were familiar with the Jewish law, which they copied out

Scourge: A whip with lots of straps which was used for beating criminals

Scroll: A roll of parchment or papyrus for writing on

Stations of the Cross: A series of fourteen images, showing the stages of Jesus' journey to Calvary

Stereotyping: Assuming things about people just because of, for example, what they look like or how they speak or how they dress

Suffix: A word which is attached to the end of another word to make a new word (eg, in the word snowboarding, 'boarding' is a suffix)

Suffragette: A woman who fought for the right of women to vote in elections

Synagogue: A building where Jewish religious services and religious teaching takes place

Tallit or Tallith: A white shawl with fringed corners worn by Jewish men during religious services

Tanach: The Hebrew Bible, divided into the *Torah, Prophets* and *The Writings*

Taskmaster: A person who oversees people doing hard, continuous work

Testament: a covenant (agreement) established between God and man

Torah: The first five books of the Hebrew Bible

Trades Union: An organisation which stands up for the rights of workers

Traitor: A person who betrays friends, country or a cause

Tumour: A bad growth inside the body

Ur: An ancient city in southern Mesopotamia (part of present day Iraq). It used to be on a coast but the city ruins are now well inland, because the coastline has changed. Abraham came from Ur.

Vocation: A special calling or urge to follow a particular career or way of life

Western or Wailing Wall: A wall in Jerusalem which was once part of the great Temple of Herod. Jews now pray at it.

Writing boards: Scribes sometimes used writing boards. These were made of wood or ivory with a writing surface covered with wax. The scribes would use an instrument to press the shapes of letters into the wax. The wax could be melted and used again.

Zealot: A nationalist group that fought the Romans in Palestine

Acknowledgements

Acknowledgements:

The authors and Colourpoint Books gratefully acknowledge the assistance of the following people and organisations:

The Church of Ireland, specially Rev W Seale and the Select Vestry of St Columba's Parish Church, Omagh
The Church of Scotland
The Gideons International
Dr Martin Melaugh, ©Cain, University of Ulster
Omagh Community Church, specially Brendan McCarthy and Marianne Maréchaux
Open Doors
Samaritan's Purse – Operation Christian Child
Sharyn Mckay: www.longlifeministries.org (*The Voice of Hope* by William and Sharyn Mckay, Ambassador Publications; ISBN 1840301724)
St Paul's (formerly St Paul's Publications) for permission to use their role-play on forgiveness.
Strathclyde University
Leprosy Mission
Wycliffe UK; John Hamilton
Rebekah Bleakley

Picture Credits:

By kind permission of the Dean of St Anne's Cathedral, Belfast: 94
©Cain (cain.ulst.ac.uk): 73 (Corrymeela sign)
Corbis: 57, 73 (Huddleston)
Design Pics: 51, 52
Getty Images: cover and frontispiece, 22, 43 (top right), 62 (bottom right), 69, 85, 95, 104
The Gideons International: 17
The Leprosy Mission: 71
iStockphoto: 11 (all), 59 (bottom right), 60 (top right), 67 (middle left), (top left), 80 (bottom left), 86 (top four), 105, 109 (right)
James Nelson: 47
Marianne Maréchaux: 97 (right)
Michael Collins: 86 (bottom right)
Norman Johnston: 45 (map), 54 (bottom)
North Wind Picture Archive: 90 (right)
Open Doors: 19
Rebekah Bleakley: 117 (top left)
Sheila Johnston: 16 (bottom right)
Strathclyde Univ: 54 (top and middle right), 55 (all)
Wendy Faris: 20 (both), 97 (left), 117 (right)
Wesley Johnston: 67 (bottom left)
Wikipedia Commons: 43 (bottom right)
Wycliffe UK: 18 (both)

Copyright has been acknowledged to the best of our ability. If there are any inadvertent errors or omissions, we shall be happy to correct them in any future editions.

Also in this series

Also available in this series of resources for the new Core Syllabus for Religious Education at Key Stage 3:

Christianity in Close-up Book 2

THE CHRISTIAN CHURCH

by Wendy Faris and Heather Hamilton

ISBN: 978 1 904242 76 5

Price: £9.99

This text covers all the important areas of Objective 1 under the main headings of The Early Church, The Church Through the Ages and The Church Today.

In the same accessible and colourful format as Book 1, it includes questions and activities which address the topics in a fresh and engaging style, helping to create active participation and enjoyment of the subject.

Resource CDs

A CD of printable activity sheets and teacher resources is available for each book. These can be printed out in the necessary numbers and distributed to the class. There are also sheets specifically for teachers which provide resources for a variety of additional practical activities.

Resource CD for Book 1

ISBN: 978 1 904242 85 7 *Price: £39.99 + VAT*

Resource CD for Book 2

ISBN: 978 1 904242 86 4 *Price: £29.99 + VAT*

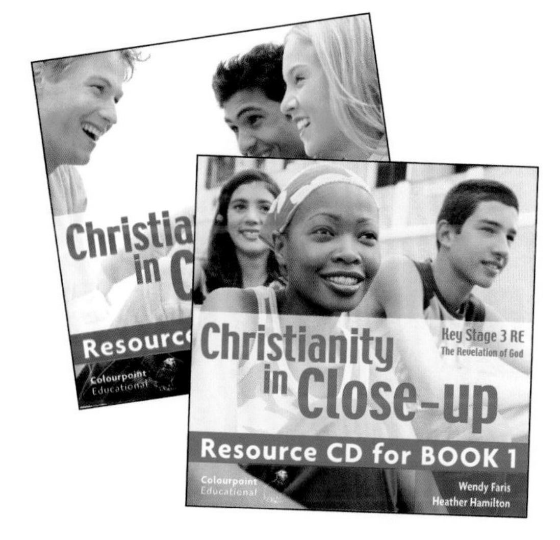

For a full range of materials available from Colourpoint Educational, visit our web site:

Web: www.colourpoint.co.uk

Or contact Colourpoint Educational at:

Tel: 028 9182 0505 Fax: 028 9182 1900

E-mail: sales@colourpoint.co.uk

Colourpoint Books, Colourpoint House, Jubilee Business Park, 21 Jubilee Road, Newtownards, Co Down, BT23 4YH

Colourpoint
Educational
SERVING EDUCATION